I

I

THE IMMUTABLE AND PERPETUAL DIVINE IN 9

DAVIDE

Library of Congress Control Number:		2018909320
ISBN:	Hardcover	978-1-9845-0137-0
	Softcover	978-1-9845-0136-3
	eBook	978-1-9845-0135-6

Print information available on the last page.

Rev. date: 08/15/2018

To order additional copies of this book, contact:
Xlibris
1-800-455-039
www.Xlibris.com.au
Orders@Xlibris.com.au
779959

CONTENTS

SOURCE
LOVE
LOVER
LOT
GODS
MATHEMATICIAN
DEITY
SUN
PHYSICS
DIVINE
RAYS
ELECTRICIAN
CURRENT
LOVE
SOURCE
OXYGEN
EGO
R
LOVER
BREATH
I
ENGINE
CARBONS
ME
DANCE
PLAY
EYES
GAMES

CHAPTER 1

OUR CONNECTIVITY AND ONENESS

> I am in your talks. I am in your sums. Eyes open,
> you'll find me in your breath. In your oxygen and carbons
> too. Are we not one?

> Devad

Dear blessed reader, there is much love and joy for everyone here in our bountiful earth. This book is dedicated to all humanity and is meant to honour those who strive to make this world a better place for everyone and all living things. My sincere thanks too for choosing to come on this journey to explore what lies ahead.

After reaching the end of this reading, it is hoped that on reflection, in the context of what is found here, the reader will be led to a clarity of what our ultimate purpose is. All the statements about to be read here have served me well in most extraordinary ways. Wholeheartedly believing in them as truths has greatly impacted my life so far, for they have given me insights into the irrefutable laws of the universe governing us.

Our connectedness is embedded in the English dialogue to make us aware that we are indeed all part of the oneness in all of us. Therefore, we do not need to imagine any more by virtue of what we have found but must wisely make every effort to become one with the one that is in all.

Everyone that is using English as a means of communication is effusing a magnanimous power in all its variation. What is discovered here will make one think twice and be very wary of how we write and speak the language that we use.

The second most important discovery is the demonstration of how the physics of working energy, through the analogy of electricity, influence our lives in a major way.

Now to kick off, English and mathematics must be seen as electricity, powering all the words written from start to finish of this narrative of life related here.

This triple play is encapsulated in Ohm's law to do with voltage, energy or current flow and resistance. According to the Oxford living dictionaries Ohm's law in physics state that electrical current is proportional to voltage and inversely proportional to resistance. This means that a flow of electricity or current will deliver the desired outcome after taking into account and allowing for any factors that constitute any resistance to its delivery.

In the relationship (IR) spoken about, I is the current flowing, and R is the resistance. How this affects our lives will make much sense later on.

Let us now create an environment where energy is freely flowing through us. We have gotten rid of all the resistance through superconductivity, which means we are allowing an immensely bright light to shine on us. Love is that powerful beam that allows it to hasten through with the live chord of these electrifying words.

CHAPTER 2

LOVE

I am in the sun and the rays in the source as I am in love and lover too.

Devad

What we are looking for is what is looking.

St Francis of Assisi

So power surges within us with no hindrance, as St Francis of Assisi put it, by looking inside us for the source of the flow. Prior to realising this, all our efforts for fulfilment all along may have been focused on the outside world, where things are always changing, creating instability for the reason that we cannot control them the way we want. So we are going to move along the wire with a light that destroys all opposition so we can stay energised.

At this point, this beautiful definition of success is a good interlude:

He has achieved success who has lived well, laughed often and loved much; who has enjoyed the trust of pure women and the love of little children; who has filled his niche and accomplished his task; who has left the world better than he found it, whether by an improved poppy, a perfect poem, or a rescued soul; who has never lacked appreciation of earth's beauty or failed to express it; who has always looked for the best in others and given them the best he had; whose life was an inspiration; whose memory a benediction. (Prize-winning definition of *success* in a contest by *Brownbook Magazine*, Boston (1904), by Bessie Anderson Stanley (1879–1952))

CHAPTER 3

TO EACH A JOURNEY

The only journey I know is the road that leads me from within.

Devad

We begin our own personal cycle on this earth from inception, the moment we enter this new world from the safety of the womb. As days go by, we get closer and closer to our mothers.

It is crucial that our mums always comfort us with their kind and gentle voices, make us feel safe against their warm bodies with plenty of hugs and kisses, and satisfy our need to get stronger to face the world with a steeled will. This is especially critical because the newborn totally relies on touch, as its eyes only begin to see clearly as the days and weeks go by.

It is also important to gradually introduce only soft sounds early in the baby's life instead of an immediate onslaught of loud, cacophonic noises. Therefore, it will be a good idea to sing softly and sweetly to the baby as often as possible.

What our parents in particular and generally all others along the way impress upon us, and the way they nurture us, may perhaps reflect on the collective impact our lives have on society. We are given insight into this important and reliable life-saving support by observing the offspring of animals and birds and their excited interactions with their mothers and their eagerness to be as close as possible to them.

Genetics play a role too, but our evolution in time and empowered resolve may alter all the characteristics we tend to believe we are hardwired with. Our prebirth disposition of having past lives and the corresponding traits we inherit may never be proved, but this life may be the platform to transform the ill-serving ones that keep us in bondage.

Generations of families may have sadly missed out on the opportunity to provide this invaluable service to mankind by way of effectively providing all the necessary love, guidance, opportunities, and discipline for the child to grow into a substantial human being. If we are not doing this, we are not aware that we are grossly negligent in rejecting a golden invitation to be exemplary parents and extraordinary hosts so that we do not leave our children wanting in all aspects of their growth.

It is never too late to reflect on our own childhood to highlight how we can start now with the new knowledge we have acquired to remedy this oversight.

This is a compelling reason for all of us to forgo the thought of entertaining excuses and blame, and to instead acknowledge that we are all here to play an active role in cementing human bonds with affection, understanding, kindness, and a generousness of the heart. It may prompt us to ask if we can judge others knowing now that we ourselves may have come with some accumulated defects and some more added along in this life.

Perhaps the sole purpose of being born here on earth is to seek perfection of the highest order before our soul discards this body for its next journey, to realise the state of just being. This could mean that our sole purpose is to peak at a vibratory level of perpetual bliss.

Our resolve to accomplish this noble goal is a test for us human beings, to challenge our shortcomings with an in-depth understanding of all our thoughts, words, and actions.

The central figure in the Gita, mindful of the fact that humanity for a large part had lost its way, prescribed the seventeen Yogas for us to practise every day to get us back on the right path to eventual self-realisation. The precepts conceptualised in these lessons present a scenario where our realisation uplifts us to celebrate life every day in all its glory, with a sense of extreme joy and peace that catapults us to euphoric heights.

We all can learn to emulate babies, with their instantaneous cheerfulness and contagious joy. Babies, with their uninhibited disposition and camaraderie amongst themselves, ooze happiness seamlessly.

This could be the prime reason we are drawn to them, because older children and adults miss that instinctive 'mindless' or 'thoughtless' exuberance and enthusiasm not nurtured in their own growth, which are so endearingly enchanting.

The central figure in the Gita, Krishna, in his life on earth, embodied a complete personality that all of us hopefully work towards before our use-by date. He was the personification of all-conquering love, sublime joy, peace, and happiness; the enjoyer and partaker of everything with no judgement, charitable and generous; and the protector of all the true freedom we all inwardly seek in our lives, even though it has always been ever-present in us but hidden by our sense attachments.

CHAPTER 4

OUR MAGNIFICENT UNIVERSE

The same magnificence, the microcosm, within.

Devad

Our cosmos with our universe, magnificent and awe-inspiring, is adorned and decorated by thousands of stars. The sky too pulses with the light and energy of our amazingly benevolent sun. Our revolving, life-giving Earth adds to the cosmic entourage. The romantic moon and a parade of distant planets immeasurably add to the beauty of the night.

Apart from paying homage to them in our romantic interludes, many of us are not aware of their individual and combined influence and effect and all-powerful impact on our lives.

The Earth revolves on its axis and orbits around the mighty sun together with all the other celestial participants, energised by the sun, to offer freely their vast and valued resources.

By some mysterious force, life abounds on Earth, sustained by the great sun, and also in some way or the other, by the moon and stars and planets and other celestial bodies.

What awe and mystery does this present for us, and what deep influences are augured for us here on Earth? What does it mean for the universe? What part does the whole universe play in all our lives? Does the significance of numbers that have been connected to the sun and planets play a part in influencing our behaviour, and does it also act as a warning guide to help us heed our ways?

Perhaps if we conduct detailed studies of the role of the sun and planets in outcomes of all events that rely on the fall of numbers, directly or indirectly, this may provide the answers. If this is conclusively proved, we may uncover a hive of clues to use for all sorts of discoveries and perhaps ultimately find cures for all known diseases.

Does the shape of our universal members and the power and force of their circuit or orbital movements define our existence by ripple, affecting our lives through our thoughts, feelings, and actions in motion, making us or breaking us? Is the whole world a stage, like William Shakespeare suggested in one of his plays, entitled *As You Like It*? Are we the actors, and is the universe cleverly, albeit with some mischief, directing our acting and choreographing our every move according to our potential and expansion?

We have seasons, one following the other, each with its own moon phases impacting what, where, when, and how we plant or sow or cultivate our crops.

'As we sow, so we reap' is significant in how, through circuitry movements, loaded energy is thrust, accumulating in each successive move our thoughts, feelings, and actions, timeless circles no one can avoid, returning again and again. This dynamism essentially carves out the choices we make with the corresponding landscape of our thoughts.

Out of desperation, we gradually become despondent as we give in to our weak thoughts. Such repetitive thoughts and actions breed habits; habits become grooved deep, like the music or songs on a gramophone record. With each successive debilitating habit, thoughts become the gaoler and the deep-cut grooves, the bars to our self-imposed prison. There seems to be no escape; the whole being loses its glitter with complaints and excuses.

For some of us, depressive feelings and mood swings become our constant companions. Through these highs and lows, our energy levels subside, and we tire quickly and become easily agitated and anxious.

Yet the answers and solutions are there, deep within us, to help all of us reclaim our rightful role in this life. We find ourselves trapped in a seemingly inexplicable situation and see no escape from the inevitable and mind-boggling phenomenon that what manifests in one ends up in one more profound than what was seeded and given growth. The doses increase in each successful circuit.

We cannot escape this continuous cycle and amazing phenomenon from the time we are born to the end of our tenure here on this earth. It is as if the clever and intelligently ingenious universe that provides all our needs and wants and nourishment for our growth and all the material wants that we could ever wish for, all the playgrounds for our games, all the intelligence for our creativity, and much more, has kept an ace up its sleeve. That no being, no matter how intelligent, how creative, or how ingenious, or with all the power and resources mustered, cannot ever escape this dynamism. It is as if the universe, with its immense power, is emulating the notion of a god through this handiwork to challenge us to be continuously creative.

It seems our whole life follows the same patterns, measured in the mechanics of a ripple. When the water is disturbed, ripples form, and after a period, the water calms again—much like most of our lives, with constant disturbances that upset our own stillness.

When we are urged to be one with God, it may mean that we be like God in every way, especially the creative aspect.

We have a tendency to fashion our beliefs according to our needs and wants and desires. We have decided that God is responsible for all our happiness and pain, and that prayer will favour us and spare us from despair and poverty and everything else that our daily lives throw at us. Or so we are led to believe. How can God be so unfair? is often asked. Some say they do not believe in God, as if God cares.

Everything, it seems, including every thought and every feeling and every action, is automatically set on automated mode through the workings of the universe from the beginning of time. This was so designed to give an equal chance to every human being to fulfil every possibility sought or every goal aspired to be reached for happiness and fulfilment in all endeavours, irrespective of the different cultures we have been brought up in.

As we are inevitably caught up in this endless cycle, this personification of life and death, we tend to forget that there are just as many opportunities or escape clauses as there are endless cycles. With the gaining of this knowledge, there is hope that we do not continually see ourselves as victims.

The Bhagavad Gita is, in essence, this message. It postulates that the transformation of our lives has its basis in the impermanence of almost every facet of our lives, and this makes sense when we begin to at last look at afflictions and pain bearers as opportunities to rise above and not dwell on them. Somehow this opportunity of insight, if grasped with both hands, culminates in a completeness of being, making a substantial difference in enhancing our humanity.

Our true heart, in most of us, becomes covered by a false heart through the layers of conditioning in making us believe that we are different from everyone else. We are led to believe that our ancestry, parents, birth, age, and a host of other markings and behavioural attributes and everything else that give us different identities are factors that make us who we are.

This is not so, because they are just tags that immerse the true, authentic person that is on the inside, the connecting energy linkage that existed even before we took on a human body, it is believed.

CHAPTER 5

OUR MAGNIFICENT EARTH

We take of the earth, before long the earth we give
back, what is it that passes?

Devad

The earth is the crown jewel in our lives, and to keep it glittering, our sum total goodness is our only chance of doing this. All our actions that are selflessly performed enable the authentic inner energy to connect every human being. This inner wisdom is the giver, keeper, and enduring sustenance of an authentic life that beautifies our human existence. The inner jewels blaze forever because true generosity profoundly empowers our lives in a way no material possessions could ever satisfy.

This holy grail of life must manifest at first in a family. When members of a family interact with sincere passion for mutual and community enrichment, they lay strong human bonds. Great foundations of strengthened human connections thrive within community organisations and institutions and social gatherings. The act of loving giving is the precursor to all other actions and thoughts that will propel us to be true and highly regarded and noble human beings.

When a family is imbued with this greater heartfelt giving and generosity of spirit, then the earth and universe respond in a like fashion when a higher consciousness manifests and lights up the world. Unbreakable ties form, and this ego-free gesture generates and gives forth warmth and a kind of spiritual love and inspires everyone to work and live selflessly.

A family unit imbued with these high qualities is the foundation for all the external gatherings and enterprises and working groups that all societies engage in and commit to in their various pursuits.

The greatest gift parents—and in particular, a mother—can give their child is sincere vocally expressed love and hugs and warm embraces that only a mother can bestow or shower on her child. Nothing else matters or can take the place of this gift of deep caring, which can be likened to Samson's colossal strength, that a mother passes on to her children.

The father too plays a significant role with his open expression of amity and care, which builds and toughens the creative will of the child with double force. Siblings learn to do likewise.

How often do we hear 'I did not need your money and everything that it could buy, all I needed was that you were there for me and reassured me with your kind and warm embrace or love', or a similar desperate cry for recognition coming out of the lips of grown-ups? This is played out in movies too, time in and time out. Adults, we would have imagined, would have moved on and discovered their own strength to build and rely on.

This ongoing human life drama emphasises the importance of open appreciation and the part it plays in forging the strength of our creative wills. This gift of giving, drawing all like a powerful magnet, is like a fountain that has its source from somewhere deep within us and that is the necessary spark in empowering families and future generations of families.

No child should be denied this tower of strength, and no excuse should rob a future generation of this all-important creative willpower of compassion.

Every child has a well of energy buoyed by different needs, and only the reassurance and guardianship from a trusted source, such as the mother, can flower meaningful expressions of this energy peculiar to each child. As the child grows, this emotional energy is not stored up within but is put to good use, thanks to this environment of trust. In this way, it may be channelled to the appropriate creative activity that will be most rewarding for the child's growth and motivation and eventual satisfaction with life as an adult.

If this emotional energy is locked in, then the body functions are compromised, and if not adversely expressed in needs, wants, ego, and anger, health may suffer instead.

This unwholesome double whammy may be avoided in the child's growth if we parents pay careful attention to the child's inclinations early on. The path best suited will be the child's choosing, which will boost self-esteem and confidence.

With this type of friendly interaction, there is a greater chance that society as a whole will be better served. Therefore, the importance of parents, next of kin, teachers, guardians, and carers can never be underestimated.

The local school parent-teacher interaction is enriched with this endearing, positive culture of giving, and it automatically and spontaneously mirrors goodwill and respect in this association. The teachers and students in these schools and universities and other institutions of higher learning are ultimately the immediate benefactors of these strong family values; in turn, society as a whole progresses with illuminating and enthusiastic participants.

People in such societies then maintain their authentic inner selves and function independently and individually but in a cohesive and unifying manner, with strong ties and understanding.

Such people enter the workforce and take their talents and skills to a new level mainly because their strong values drive them to give their best without compromise. They have no inhibitions and no baggage to stymie their enthusiasm, so they are able to contribute to the better good; the act of giving spurs them to greater heights.

Business enterprises and institutions with such a workforce will, in turn, foster strong family values, knowing and appreciating that mutual benefit can be the only outcome. Organisations' policies and rules and regulations will then be formulated with mutual respect and interdependence with a bilateral view, with a proactive creed giving the workers voices and confidence to function at their best, creating healthy environments. This power to the workforce is recognition that trustworthiness and faith cement relationships, and this act of giving brings the greatest rewards.

When the material and spiritual needs of people are met, forward movement is not hindered but abounds with potential energy for great outcomes.

It is commended that many institutions and organisations actively participate in raising money for charities, welfare groups, and community service providers.

To allay the suspicion that these institutions engaging in acts of charity are superficial philanthropists with self-interests and that promotion of their wares is the chief motive driving these acts of charity, noble and ethical practices must go hand in hand to foster truthfulness.

If ever any organisations were seen to be intimidating and threatening employees with dismissal through archaic rules and regulations, it would serve them and humanity better if they were fostering a culture of tolerance and sincere interdependence. This will uplift and energise the workforce to perform enthusiastically and diligently. Sincere praise does wonders for self-esteem and confidence, just as criticism destroys the spirit.

There is a way of managing a few to a few hundred to thousands of people that have differing perceptions and views and opinions and ideas. The seemingly simplistic but, we believe, not by any means ingenious way is not to manage but to get everyone on the side of common sense. By giving respect and by endowing everyone with self-worth through self-analysis and intuition are priceless. To see difficulties and difference of opinions as mutual opportunities to bond closely for the same outcomes. Most of all, truthfulness will generate goodwill, and issues will always be dealt with compassion.

Self-management will be a winner for both the employer and employees. Every worker or employee will have taken the role of leadership in a way. A culture of self-rule will engender independence and disciplines that will foster commitment.

If ever there are any transgressions, open admission will result because employees are treated with respect and a mutual acknowledgement that to err is human.

Giving—a generosity of the heart, mind, thought, actions, words, deeds, and spirit, generosity to oneself by overlooking looks, body, and shape—shifts the focus away from being judgemental. As a result of this genuine warmth of heart, we perceive everyone to be generous and kind, and if ever, any alienation is fleeting and temporary, not what our inner selves are.

The idea of free will—to operate unhindered with cumbersome restrictions that inhibit productivity and stifle innovativeness and creativity, and that which accumulates mental strife and negativity—is then fostered for common good.

We never escape this kind of peer pressure from childhood, and this detracts from the untainted innocence of the self. The solution lies in actively and energetically involving the different levels of management and workforce for their input for all-round worker improvement. All staff, by their own realisation, will acknowledge that they need to take a closer look at all sides of themselves with a 'mirror, mirror' approach to identify and freely admit they are acting their false selves if ever their behaviour is called into question.

Companies and all institutions of employment, big and small, are where their employees spend the greater part of their time. Prudence on the part of these companies and institutions will ensure their longevity if workers are more like family members, working together to keep the family strong.

We often ponder the reasons we act and behave robotically, as if our essential selves have deserted us or as if we may have lost cognisance of our true selves. This makes it seem as if we have tampered with ourselves and ended up dangled, like puppets on a string with no self-control.

Through this action, we have taken many false personalities in one. We have the ego personality, the main culprit, the daddy of all devils. The want personality and the need personality and, of course, the denial personality—they are the support personalities for the ego personality. From these displays emerge the bad guys of the acquired trio of personalities.

The arch-enemy is anger. It consumes and devours humanity; it dehumanises us and results in an army of seemingly soulless people afflicted by a malady that is ignored or overlooked invariably with manufactured excuses so far from the truth.

The foundation of family life from the beginning of our human existence, loving and giving has been the cornerstone of the family bond. For generations, women were the gatherers; they gave their wholehearted attention and devotion to keep the home fires burning. Men, the hunters, provided food and creature comforts. Up to this day, the nurturing and care of the children by the mums and dads, the family fabric, has survived amidst all the problems faced and all the obstacles life throws at it.

More so now than ever, families have to be strong together, and this has to be stepped up to counteract the pitfalls of our fast-accelerating technological advancement.

It is the give factor that keeps on giving. Giving adds, and taking detracts. Giving accumulates and goes forward; taking goes backwards and takes away from. Living in the giving imbues one with an enormous power that lifts one's spirits the only way giving can. If every word, thought, and action are in a forward move, more power is resourced.

The most effective tool in enhancing and empowering our mental and physical prowess is illustrated in our daily lives, for when we set out to do something, we have already automatically imagined a picture of that action long before it is performed, whether we know it or not.

People cannot be forced to be nice to one another; an environment has to be created which is conducive to good vibrations that spread to one and all. Every time a word of some negative slant is expressed, what seems to be really coming to the fore is some really deep need or want known or we are unaware of.

This is an opportunity that is constantly presented to us—the opportunity to take a closer look at ourselves to remedy our disenchantment. To live a richly authentic life is only possible if we tune in to our inner wisdom. How do we differentiate between true inner self and all the other selves that get in the way, obstructing the emergence of this powerful light of life?

Both our heart and mind emotions are corrupted with external environmental influences and belief systems that pervade and obstruct our own insight and discoveries. We are also bombarded with faulty information from birth, to such an extent that the false identity overlaps and alternates with the true identity.

The false identity is the data that makes up who we are—age, parents, friends, looks, and so on—that help hide the truth of who we are on the inside, the self we were born to before the layers of interlopers. If the head, where all ideas emerge from, is heavy with biased information, all else that follows evolves from shaky foundations.

Leadership is not only cleverly or intelligently assessing and acting accordingly to the best advantage presented to gain ascendency for various gains. It is a mark of outstanding leadership where the human perspective is just as important to create an environment where we have eagerly willing and enthusiastic people engaging in meaningful and value-adding chores. This intelligence of good vibrations sets the patterns and examples of grand mateships.

In this way, people will inherently know what the boundaries are and will act and behave accordingly. Respect earned will determine that, just like good captains, they guide their own ships.

All our actions point to that. When you add to anything, the thing increases, as opposed to when you take from something, which diminishes it. It depletes completely if the taking from something is continued and not abated, because the minus factor changes it completely to something that is not itself any more.

We wonder if all our sciences of mathematics—addition and subtraction and multiplying and dividing—actually hold greater meaning for our well-being than just budgeting and other mundane but essential financial activities that many of us are experts at.

To sum it up (no pun intended), forward thoughts and actions and backward thoughts and actions are the see-sawing of our lives in an endless fashion.

How do we know we have a perfect or false self? Our entire body and all its parts, our actions, and our thoughts and emotions will somehow, in more ways than one, cry out and, in a multitude of ways, reveal the false self or selves, knowing that, in sufferance, they are oppressing the true self. When the false self in us is in denial, anger manifests; ego, needs, wants, a temper, and a tirade of emotions are spit out.

The movie of our minds is played out day after day, and when we are not asleep, traffic of never-ending thoughts pass by, a cavalcade of highs and lows constantly on the move. All the while, our all-important energy levels dwindle, and our cells are deprived of their ordained activity to keep us alive.

The puppetry of thoughts parades endlessly, gradually grooving into our psyche, and cuts deep dents in our minds, which eventuates in hard-to-break cemented habits that anchor our thoughts in a spiralling overture of delusional dimensions, cacophonic to the inner spirit to make its presence felt.

This gradual alienation of our inner core by this foreign legion of tricksters overtakes and overwhelms us. We seem powerless to escape from these fetters for our salvation, but we should be hard-pressed to escape these claws that so tightly grip us.

We have to traverse a million or more words in many books of varied subjects and topics, and search high and low for a way that can get to the core of our being in spite of all our shortcomings and in spite of any impediments—mental, spiritual, or cultural—or any other bias or prejudice. Our search for the meaning of life is never-ending, but we will be better served if we endeavour to become free of any restrictive forces.

Every book ever written, every tale ever told, and every song ever sung is a pointer for us; it is the result of some deep need from some deep place we know not of as yet, but it is put out there to make us richer for our own quest and growth. All our expressions are so sourced.

There is a certain inherent power when one seeks to get to the heart of anything, and it is pure and whole; certainly so when anyone seeks to identify with this depth of the human fire of creativity, likened to the heat of the inner heart of a fiery volcano.

This fire of creativity within has its counterpart, the mighty sun without, which is a constant reminder of its immense potential force.

Chapter 6

OUR ABUNDANCE

Bountiful grace flows in a myriad ways to the heart
that seeks the sun's rays.

Devad

So we are all looking inwards and lit by the powerful sun that shines its bright rays on us. Now we are able to declare:

I am here to experience this earthly life as the brightest star, ever sparkling with the radiance of the sun.

I have a picture-perfect imagination, envisioning all the abundance I truly desire. I have been endowed with inventiveness and innovative abilities to magically transcend all impediments and to master design my preferred lifestyle.

I may have forgotten or do not know what the purpose of my life is, but now there is ever-available guidance for me to set forth towards this aspect of my journey. I know, with gratitude and appreciation, that the universe's intention is only my best interests.

I am equipped to tap into the vast abundances of the cosmos ever available to me. I am the deity; I am divine, as I am the source. I am love; I am the lover.

I am the only creator that can satisfy all my desires, wants, needs, and all that I seek and believe will fulfil me. I love myself for who I am, as I am always true to myself.

Having reflected on all this that I have read, now I know what I could do to enable me to live my life fully.

We know and have acknowledged that our love sparks the ever-flowing power supply of the sun and embellishes the source within all of us to stay strong and formidable against all impediments of the R world.

I slay all Goliaths.

Along the way, these charged electrical wires of our lives sometimes encounter the very narrow pipes of straining pressure in the ways of beliefs that thwart our strongest push to ride above them.

Here we need the fire in the heat of our resolve to burn and destroy all the narrow tubes of stubbornness and rewire, with renewed energy in our flow. Let the sparks fly to avoid short-circuiting our determination.

Chapter 7

BELIEFS

I am in the 'I' and I am in the 'R', in the OM, OHM
and MHO too.

Devad

Look well into thyself; there is a source of strength
which will always spring up if thou wilt always look.

Marcus Aurelius
(Roman emperor from 0161,
famous for his work *Meditations*)

From what was just read, it seems a plausible observation, and
it is hard not to concur that we are always receiving guidance from
within, especially now that we know energy is constantly flowing, like
the beating of our hearts.

If, for any reason, belief systems get in the way, with all that has
just been expressed, then it is now time to search deeply within to seek
out where all our emotional currents emanate from. If pain is endured
but not suffering, then a little door has opened for a comforting peek
from the outside. Pain could be dropped too, with a committed focus
to look for answers inwardly so the outside resistance dissipates.

Undergoing both suffering and pain means the fibres of the R
factor are constricted by some residues of hardened beliefs. Clashes
from opposing conduits of life forces are telling on both our thought
processes and our bodies, like limp, ineffective power in the cells of

our batteries. The frustrating ohm may have its heels dug in deep, making it hard to strengthen voltages to heighten what were voiced.

The telling play of the power of electrical energy may feel like it is hogwash, but before this book is discarded, a little tolerance may lead to a discovery of compelling reasons to reconsider. This joyful exuberance wired in me with pulsating vigour electrifies me to connect to enlighten the whole world.

When it is figured out that these are *truths*, then we are ready to come home after our tenure here on earth ends. Once the antiflow factor, R, has been obliterated, then we are switched on to now focus on our inherent creativity, with no power leakage to weaken our resolve.

CHAPTER 8

CREATION AND CREATIVITY

> There's beauty and awe in the vast expanse of the mind, even greater, still to be magically sculptured for the sheer thrills.
>
> Devad

We are now all unencumbered dynamos for all possible creations, the creators we are meant to be.

Much has been written, expounded, and experienced by multitudes through our essential and unique faculty of intentional manifesting. All living things, including us humans, are forever in a continuous cycle of making something, whether we are conscious of it or not. We and the plant and animal kingdoms never stop or cease our creativity, intentionally or not.

Whether we realise it or are aware of it or not, the very thoughts we are having right this moment have just been brought into existence. It is all to do with the free flow of electricity in full force. Similarly, our words and actions are charged to do the same.

Even with our interactions with animals and plants, mutually beneficial creativity is taking place. Existence is the constant process of that ingenuity, that instinctive, generative power within all living things.

If our orientation is driven by our needs to accomplish eventual goals, we may not feel as fulfilled with their achievements as we believed, because forced actions subjugate our natural inventiveness. However, if they are directed by our inbuilt resourcefulness—the hallmark of our living world—we will naturally delight in our achievements.

CHAPTER 9

THE MYSTERY OF LIFE

How do I go from whence I came, so not to return to this pain? See that light, reach, embrace, be it. I've come home.

Devad

Now here is a little bit of my journey on my way to discovering my purpose through finding the engine that amps up my passion.

For almost my entire adulthood, the meaning of life was always a quest on my mind, a mystery that somehow had to be solved on this earthly journey. Now at last, there is a peace in me. All my long hours, days and nights of digging, have finally paid off.

After much consideration and an urging in my soul, an innermost desire to share my discoveries has made me write this story. Ever since then, it has been my fervent passion to hasten to this momentous day in my life.

For, dear reader, it is imperative to wholeheartedly consider the implications of ignoring the hidden essence of our expressions every time breath is given to words.

It must be that we are wired to the divine and are continually bringing creations to the fore as we communicate. The inner machine must be the I ego, and the outside motormouth must be the R ego.

Chapter 10

EGO

I am an 'in' Ego OM and an 'out' ego OHM too.

Devad

I have lived on the lip of insanity, wanting to know reasons.
Knocking on a door. It opens. I have been knocking from the inside.

Rumi

For many decades, this was the story of my life. The unnecessary suffering pained me incessantly. Outwardly, there was a coolness in me that thoroughly enjoyed all the trappings of my sensual roles and role plays. Inside me, the turmoil never ceased, surfacing in a myriad of forms.

Fortunately, wild aggression was never part of my make-up, for there were outlets to be found in many forms of activities for a robust and competitive life. In me, there is always a fire that is easily stirred up with whatever passion that engages me, but for reasons unknown to me, they mostly danced in my mind.

This passion has always been integral to my satisfaction with life but was left unattended for so long through a false identity. Regrettably, ego—a noble word if viewed, acknowledged, and engaged in as the true perspective—was compensating for uneasiness for a long time.

Growing up in an environment that was deeply tribal—culturally, socially, and politically—required great strength of wit.

My desire not to leave myself open to be bullied found me seeking the company of those that commanded respect, mainly for safety in their physical presence.

Politics was clearly not for my ego self. The imagined and dreamed utopia that was fought for was quickly dashed by the self-interests and agendas of most of the leadership of the groups in those dark times.

A search for that missing something in my life often found me in bookstores and libraries, always seeking that elusive ingredient that would hopefully satisfy my great need. Perusing scores of books on a variety of topics, including how to be rich and dozens or more of other how-to subjects, really inspired me to continue in my quest. Even to this day, after I realised where this has brought me after all my researches, much more mysteries are waiting to be discovered.

This awareness that within me is the source, the place where everything is eternal, has been a real blessing. This is what St Francis was alluding to in his saying that 'what we are looking for is what is looking'. We seek fulfilment everywhere else, but in an instant, with eyes turning inwards in a timeless and spaceless moment, we are in that noiseless quiet.

So too did Yumi when he said that he had been standing for so long, trying to find what he was searching for on the outside instead of putting his focus on the inside.

The Internet too is a sign that we are all consciously becoming dependent on a super communication vehicle for all manner of things. We are going inwards to find whatever our requirements are that drive our thirst for knowledge. It is an extraordinary, life-changing facet in our lives if we consider that, in under a second, a search on the word *love* can bring up more than 8,560 million results.

Prior to the Net, libraries were the place for books for any purpose, with a huge expense of time and effort. But today, with the looking-in factor for knowledge, we must give credence to the power of our intuition. We are not just a mass but a living body in every cell, more like an electrical current with a flow that ignites our curiosity.

We are all privy to this inner information, direct from the source, for our welfare and well-being.

Unfortunately, many of us do not pay much attention to our intuitive gut feeling that is trying to point us in the right direction. The extreme unpleasantness within me would have had a transformation decades ago had attention been given to and had I acted upon what my inner voice told me many times. Constant messages failed to be interpreted because my belief systems kept brushing them aside.

Why this behaviour of repeatedly sabotaging all calls from some unknown place, these much-needed interventions? Why this strong opposition to something that could help?

It can only be attributed to my strongly ingrained ego attitude, which imposed limitations, imagined what they indicated to me, made them seemingly illusory and impossible, and just brushed them aside. After much reflection on what could have been, there is no doubt that reason points to this obnoxious impersonator that we allude to as the ego of the mind. My failure to realise the error of my ways made it become my constant obstructer.

On hindsight, my objective self was so deeply a part of me, chiefly because conscious duels within myself sought reason and logic to triumph. This caused a false pride to be stamped in me. For a long time, nothing could remove this blight, an affliction and curse that curtailed my salvation.

However, there were many instances when, fortunately, that attitude took a back seat and my inner feelings were given just a speck of attention, which resulted in much elation. Life is always wishing the best for us, and if gut feelings are not given some deep thought, much suffering may be incurred.

It makes sense now when there is often advice that any pain should be embraced; there is a lesson here that better choices could be made the next time. The presumption is that acutely knowing oneself through inward reflection could eventually awaken an awareness of the true self.

Importantly, the perspective and perception of everyone we meet could also provide clues for further analysis for self-improvement. This is the real gaining of knowledge, to improve lifestyles and better serve humanity at large.

In the Hindu philosophy, Vedanta, ego is a thought pattern that magnifies self-ignorance to the extent that everything in one's life is believed to be rationally orientated. This is a rigid bar to information, knowledge, or acknowledgement of the mystery and magic of life.

CHAPTER 11

EGO NIGHTMARE

The 'I' that I am has been blindly forsaken by my eyes
pointing outwards only.

Devad

There is one incident that is worth recounting that has imprinted
in me the importance of following my instincts. Most certainly, ego
was the master.

During days of courtship, my fiancée and I spent Friday evenings
together. On one such fine evening, my now wife helped me put
together a selection of horses to place a jackpot bet on in the next
day's horse racing card. The jackpot is where the winners of the last
four races must be selected.

On this particular race day, it was great to head to the Greyville
Racecourse in Durban to both purchase the ticket and watch all the
races. Having written out the ticket with our selections, I joined the
queue to validate our selections.

While in the line to the cashier, over the loudspeaker came
the news that the hot pot favourite, King's Palace, was backed to
prohibitive odds. This was one of the horses that we ignored when
putting together our numbers for our chance to win.

In my wanting-to-win mindset, the thought occurred to me to
replace number 14, which we chose, with number 1, which was
King's Palace. After this was done I rushed out and headed back to
the long ticket line.

Lo and behold, immediately in front of me was a huge number 14 glaring at me, blazed across the back of a long white coat worn by one of the racecourse attendants. My inner being signalled to me to write a new ticket and to revert to the original numbers chosen the night before.

Resistance became my worst enemy. Number 14 was paying more than $20. How can it possibly beat 1, which was at 'cannot lose' odds? So now, to change or not to change was my predicament. Soon hesitation found me at the window, and my choice was made for me.

As I watched the horses stride out to the starting stall for this particular race, to rub salt in my wounds, 14 strode out first in a fast canter. The saddleclothed 1 was the last to find its way to the starter. It was too late when an outer sign to change presented itself to me, and now the horses themselves gave me a preview of my pain. The suffering was unbearable, and it was self-incurred too, to make it more torturous.

More pain was inflicted on me when my worst fear took form. An identical scene played out, and the result was the same when the outsider, number 14, romped home and King's Palace placed last. My suffering continued when the payout for the winning jackpot was $6,000, and my ego took a tumble.

There were many incidents that have occurred that made me appreciate how important it is to realise and acknowledge that a greater force has all our backs throughout all our lives. We are constantly reminded, spurred, urged, and encouraged to get back on the path to become one—to be immersed in a dazzling light, to be shining stars eternally.

By the way, the name of the horse that won was Fitzgerald, with a little embarrassment. Urban Dictionary gives its meaning as 'a man being caught with his pants down'. Humorous as it is, nonetheless, it is an excruciating memory to recall.

Intuition may be best explained as leaving all options open and then acting on a hunch through various signs presented—a strong gut feeling. These are subtle ways. Initially, it is a bit difficult to get a grip on unless the ego is zeroed in on. It is an art that can be tuned in to if an effortless life flow is allowed. Turning inwards for guidance is the key, instead of totally relying on the material-sense urges only.

CHAPTER 12

EGO TOOK A BACK SEAT

Sweet grace must unfold for the eyes have turned inwards.

Devad

There is another story I feel must be told to demonstrate how life directs us in various and illuminating ways. This was an incident that took place when I was driving to the same racecourse mentioned in my previous episode in Durban.

It was Saturday morning. I had punting on my mind, thinking as usual about how good it would be if some winners would emerge in my selections. Since the turf track was under four hundred metres from my unit building, walking there was an easy breeze. However, I had an inkling that the first race was a good time to start the day. Driving there on that day would ensure a chance to pick a winner to start the day with a bang.

As I neared my destination, there on the sidewalk a few metres in front of me, a despicable crime was taking place. Before me, a cowering man was being attacked by a pickpocket trying to relieve him of his wallet. *Hoot, hoot,* my car horn screamed repeatedly as I slowed the car down to almost a standstill.

Victory was in sight when the assailant let go of the frightened victim on the ground and ran off like a scared dog. The lucky person got back on his feet, waved his hand in appreciation as he brushed himself, and walked on. Likewise, after my thumbs up to him, I proceeded on my way.

Before the commencement of the first race, a quick glance at the race book became a very prolonged look of surprise and astonishment. Something within me lit a few light bulbs in my head. Blinking a few times did not change what was staring right at me.

After rushing to the ticket centre, firmly pushing any doubts and procrastinations aside, I placed a $100 win-and-place ticket on the horse that caught my fixed attention.

My excitement made me yell when my providential pick hit the finish line first. I was jumping for joy, thrusting my fist in the air, and clutching the ticket worth a cool $1,000.

The name of the dam of this particular horse was—you guessed it—Pickpocket.

Acting on my hunch at once smoothly ensured that ego was not given an opportunity to intervene this time. Remembering my earlier quick impulse to help the distraught pedestrian, I was touched and offered deep appreciation for this fortuitous happening.

On reflection, many incidents come to mind where creativity happened after the intention was set, enacting the visual outcomes with imagination and colour, allowing life to play out the details as if they were a reality.

CHAPTER 13

THE TV CABINET

All that we are is a result of what we thought.

Gautama Buddha

Amongst the many experiences, my indulging in creativity with the magical manifestation process really amazes me. One such story has to be told.

On one such inspired feeling, my determination to build a television cabinet from scratch just for the joy of it grew. The design, colour, and cost were already worked out in my head, as this idea had been brewing for a while. All these images were transferred to paper, with all measurements worked out, shaded in black.

A black cabinet, which I visualised with a smile, as if my television were sitting on it in my living room, made a striking picture. It satisfied me even more when I imagined the other features that would sit on it—included were the hi-fi sound system and colourful ornaments. The picture was perfect.

This print in my mind accompanied me everywhere—when I was walking, on the train, at work, and everywhere my day or night took me.

About three months later, it was my turn to choose six numbers for a lotto syndicate at work. The syndicate had an entry for the Monday draw. Four of us, close work colleagues at David Jones at Chatswood, got together each morning before the night's draw to confirm our selections.

On the night before my numbers were to be handed in for the syndicate's permutation, thoughts of the likely numbers played in my mind, a few moments at a time.

All that I remembered in the morning on the train to work was a hazy recollection of some fish falling from a hole in the sky. Gradually, pieces of my dream began to emerge, and the picture appeared to me in some detail.

It was like an ocean in the clouds, spitting out these flailing creatures which landed at the doorway of the kitchen we used to cook and dine in all those decades ago. I was ten years old so it was becoming tiring handing these slippery shad to all our neighbours and passers-by continuously. Then the alarm clock intruded both my dream and sleep.

My mind immediately raced with inventive thoughts, as numbers and my dream seemed somehow connected. Memories emerged of those earlier years in Durban, when our evening pastime was placing money on a numbers story game popular in the seventies. Drinking beer, talking racing, and having a flutter in this intriguing sport where stories were told, we had to follow the thread for over five days. Each evening, it revealed clues in the story of what numbers to play to win six shillings at a tickey a punt. Fahfee or Fafi, the name of the game, came with a dream guide where the numerals 1 to 36 stood for different objects.

Recalling my dream in numbers through the Fafi guide led me to come up with my six numbers for our lotto permutation. Two of the numbers chosen as my pick included 3, which was big water (ocean), and 13, which was big fish.

When I was home that evening, my excited anticipation was rewarded, for the winning lotto balls that fell that night included my six numbers, which filled the second division prize. The TV cabinet that was envisioned, passionately intentioned three months ago, and sustained for this time could now become a reality.

A month later, my project came to fruition and panned out exactly as my mind imagined it. Oh, yes, the lotto share for me was $350, almost the same amount that the total cost for the fixture was calculated at when my desire to build it first arose.

The universe awaits to rejoice in us and to see us all shine through all our magnificent fabrications.

Next is my take on the relevance of the Hawaiian *Ho'oponopono*, which translates to 'correction by cleaning'.

On first thinking of its effectiveness, it's not hard to knock its practice as something ridiculous or silly. It is so easy to judge, looking at it superficially; it would be too easy to be prompted to be its executioner too. Hopefully, understanding beyond our limitations will reveal its profoundness, to be seen as it was intended and to be understood in order to change lives to vibrate at the highest.

CHAPTER 14

HO'OPONOPONO

The only task in your life and mine is the restoration
of our Identities—our Minds—back to their original state
of void or zero.

I'm sorry. Please forgive me. I love you. Thank you.

Ihaleakala Hew Len, PhD

Dr Ihaleakala Hew Len, PhD, a psychologist living in Hawaii,
devised what to me is one of the greatest mantras of four very
amazingly impactful statements. It is the most profound way of
tuning in to our higher selves to activate the power within.

Ho'oponopono translates to having the function of cleansing
our previous mental library of transgressions. When uttering these
words, our attention is turned inwards, away from the outside noise.
Len called it a new way of looking at ourselves by connecting to our
'self i-dentity '.

The key in this mantra opens the door to the sources and causes
of all that we are currently at odds with. On repeated examination
and penitence for the causes of our suffering and pain, a connection to
our inner guidance is gradually made. This impact is life-changing,
as it allows our intuition to be effortlessly activated for the flow of life,
like a river on its meandering way.

For me, it is a meditation that is priceless, because it penetrates
and destroys all remnants of our conceited persona.

The very first proclamation, 'I'm sorry', is instantly humbling in
its utterance, as much as 'Please forgive me' purifies it. Purity is the

essence of grace. When these words flow out, humble acceptance opens up to declare that all are of our choosing. Our lack of insight and understanding that everything emanates from the universal electrical presence stifle us. Being part of that, we are builders ourselves.

Judgement takes many forms, subtly hidden in our emotive feelings and ignorance. We are totally responsible and ought to be dutifully charitable for the greater good. Only love and compassion, with appreciation of all manifestations as part of life's experiences, complete our wholeness, not to pity but to support. This focus on those aspects of ourselves that we hitherto believed were externally influenced will prove to be transformational.

If these divinely directed words healed hardened inmates in a prison block in Hawaii, according to Hew Len, then reciting this prayer with conviction must be very powerful.

For those that are interested in chanting these words, repeating them many times at any time will greatly help. Ensure that 'I'm sorry, please forgive me' are the first words to be said, as they have the magic in them. If we wish to also use all the wellness benefits for others, then the focus should be on their names as we meditate for their welfare.

As we reflect on these self-cleansing words while they are being said, our dense ego energies will gradually dissipate. Long-held views and judgemental inclinations thin out, creating expansion in our lives.

It is said that after a while, when a graceful disposition becomes us, healing others too will be possible. Our higher charged energy can affect the well-being of all persons whose names are included individually with repetition of Hew Len's gems.

When we are the inner light of love and compassion, all eventualities can manifest. When we reach a zero-memory state to allow grace to flow in, the doorway to the spirit within is open.

In electrical jargon, it is like clearing all the copper pipes of all the R dirt of what we created to power intuition.

My excitement is building to a fever pitch for what the divine 9 is going to reveal to us in the later chapters that follow.

CHAPTER 15

MEDITATION FOR SEAMLESS INTEGRATION

Quiet, quiet the noises too, the commotion, the thought, stillness reigns, cellular, head, heart to feet.

Devad

Let a man lift himself by his own self alone, let him not lower himself; for this self is the friend of oneself and this self alone is the enemy of oneself.

The Bhagavad Gita

Hopefully, meditation is the medium that can take us to the depth of our existence and beyond. Meditation has been popularised throughout the world in its many forms largely because of its mysticism and offer of innumerable benefits.

Conversely, it has been taken lightly and ignored too by many because of its association with religion and gurus aided by a superficial understanding.

Meditation may be the key to reversing all damaging and destructive habits permanently. The medium of meditation could aid in inculcating good habits to overhaul ingrained unhealthy or unwanted habits. Acknowledgement of our imminent demise by design is the important halfway house to the knowledge that awaits us and that the trickery of our thoughts had for so long hidden from us.

Meditation and the widely unknown act of its practice has for too long been given divergent pathways, sometimes losing its soul and spirit in the mix, culminating in so many variations of yoga according to as many interpretations. As a result, many are ignorant or misinformed of its relevance and importance in today's hectic, pressured style of living.

Judging by the different schools of thought that exist, the benefits promised by these well-being and body and spirit and health welfare schools all may have their intended results to a certain degree if a complete equilibrium and wholeness of body, mind, and spirit has not been achieved, as was intended in the creation of meditation. However, it is highly commendable that people, for whatever reason, are imparting this very ancient art by making its potential benefits known to the wider world.

If the practitioners have the slightest doubt of where they are in this stage of their lives, then meditation in the various offered forms has somehow let slip its sparkle and heart of gold. Perhaps what has been sought remains unfulfilled, and we have not been open or aware of what meditation is all about according to the ancient originators, reputed to be well over five thousand years ago. Once understood, it will enrich us enormously, and its practice will enliven everyone to wonder at its simplicity for offering so much more to the value of our lives than ever thought of or imagined in all aspects of our human existence.

It is amazing how versatile we can become in every facet of our life when knowledge becomes the domain of everyone, especially when the true shining jewel of meditation becomes part of us. How is this to be? Why is meditation so powerful? we may well ask.

A mind that is forever a melting pot of thoughts—cycling and recycling comments and criticisms and wants and needs, highlighting and reflecting on external events and happenings and dramas and movies and the media, agitated and tormented—it gets out of control and loses power.

This misalignment creates stresses that trigger feelings and emotions that damage the self-esteem and confidence. It saps us of all the energy, and when we feel burnt out, we leave ourselves open to all kinds of influences that undermine health and self-worth.

This imbalance leaves us open and prone to diseases, disillusionment, anger, and frustration, which lead to highs and lows and make us open to depressive feelings. When we succumb to this kind of pressure, then it becomes part of us. Habits cut deep, like the grooves or troughs of a house's tin roof.

How can we remain the same self that is one with our inner being?

If we cannot recall, our parents—especially our mum—will recall our earliest years: a treasured baby and toddler and child, blissful laughter and joy, and endless moments of fun, frolic, and mischief that the whole family enjoyed.

Over time we have become what we are not. Alas, now we have welcomed a stranger to disguise our real self, who we certainly once knew, to become what we think we are. Illusion is a deceitful mirror that faces us now, a monkey sitting on our back, a usurper that wears our crown, an alien that now sits on the throne.

What is now required to rid us of this malady is an open admission and acceptance that we have indeed lost our way. Only then will we realise the folly of our ways and urgently seek to make amends to rise up to our true selves. A calming of the mind, coupled with relaxation, is now required—a prerequisite to meditation.

It is a slow process initially, but through practice and many hours of contemplation and reflection, there will be a transformation from irrational thoughts to complete calm, like a ship tossed about in a tempestuous sea that at last reaches calm waters—a resurgence of lost energy and eventual peace and an inward presence of joy and ecstasy and happiness that will last us our lifetime.

How is this possible, that a mere 'thoughtlessness' can turn a tide?

Like everything, like a habit, unyielding repetition gives strength and power and invincibility to those that are single-minded, with a determination to reach the pinnacle, come hell or high water. Simultaneously, this seeds the future achievement with a very graphic visualisation, making it a reality long before the victory is achieved. The baby in us comes to the fore, acting naturally; this is perceptual intelligence in itself, a precursor to knowledge of the self.

A guardian of the true self is ever-ready and alert to any intrusive thought, seeking out any clandestine intention to inhabit the mind and body to enslave us. This ingrained perception, like a security sensor, is ever alert, a 24/7 presence of mind sharpened and poised for action.

As we realise the importance of this ever-ready alertness, we become more acutely aware of the forces all around and about us that spell danger the moment we let our guard down. Everybody and everything that invades our senses should be eyed and viewed with caution.

This is by no means inviting paranoia—contrary to it.

To put this in perspective, consider the following questions: How many people do we come across every single day? How much advertising do we come across on our way to work or on our daily travels? How many newspapers, different types of magazines, or print media do we read or peruse weekly? How much radio news and views do we listen to daily? How much music do we listen to day and night? How much television do we watch when we are at home?

The moment these questions are asked, we begin to realise how easily we can be influenced if we let our guard down. Now we can see the enormous mountains of sense invaders that we encounter every day or night that we are awake. At once, we can see the urgency in examining all input data to counteract and destroy all offenders before they are given a window of opportunity even for a casual visit. It is imperative that we spit them out quickly.

Now it is by no means an easy feat to ward off all thoughts by mere alertness or presence of mind. It takes much more than effort; it is only possible through the presumption that we have no unfinished business, in that all our needs and wants have been satisfied.

This means that by this stage in our lives, we have set realistic goals and we have fully explored where our creative or constructive needs and wants are fountaining from. Most of all, as far as we can, we must fulfil all the desires we have.

Or, having searched our souls, we must acknowledge that our needs and wants will not dissipate, as they are just there, and they pop up from time to time for no apparent reason. Time may remedy this if we persist in our practice, for we may be overcoming an ingrained habit or something carried from our past life (this is open to conjecture if numerology is denied as a science).

If we perpetually or almost so fantasise about anything, then if it is possible, it is imperative to get into the real thing doubly fast, as there is no time like the present.

Denial serves no good purpose, and here too we must really dig deep and embolden ourselves to accept the consequences because it is a terrible and self-defeating offender when it surfaces. Ego, as mentioned before, is a bad guy and must not be approached.

Our constructive or creative needs and wants are not bad if we have a time range for assessing the resources and if we explore all our creative forces and acquire all the skills to accomplish them. This will definitely do wonders for our confidence and self-esteem and self-worth.

But ego is the total sorcerer, for it is the mind's worst trickster and destroyer. In lifting us above ground level, it puts our heads in the clouds and deeper in delusion land.

Ego is the greatest deceiver that separates and keeps apart human beings. It is that which discriminates and antagonises, and which is in itself a separatist, defining and marking imaginary borders and fences. Also categorising humans according to their attributes and power and wealth or so-called classes or lineage, amongst other falsities that have brought about constant struggles amongst peoples and nations. That which has brought about wills ill-conceived and misdirected, causing wars that impoverish and cause annihilation and destruction and mindless slaughter of whole generations.

The I factor reigns supreme, and no one knows any better. 'It is my way or not at all.'

The complete demonisation of peoples ensues, and we count the costs through compounding human misery and a depletion of the fundamental basic rights of fellow human beings. Ego sends forth its bedmates, greed and corruption, which have beset whole nations and continue to do so. Ego and its upstarts come in multitudes of disguises.

People inflicted with ego caused by ill-conceived fears constantly boost their images by alluding to connections, relatives, and even friends that are well educated, professionals with high-end jobs, or people who hold some sort of power or are somehow very rich or hold important positions in communities and institutions.

This ownership props the perpetrators in a way that we are taken in before we know it, and we fall prey to this manoeuvre; sadly, before we realise this and become wise to it, we become participants in perpetrating the sham.

The other effect on the listener or observer is that it diverts our thoughts to our own visions of grandeur that sublimate us. We see ourselves as inferior in some way or the other, and the rot of needs and wants is played out once again.

Whole generations fall prey to this, and the ensuing issues seem to preoccupy the mind and leave it open to falsity. Once again, habits detrimental to mental strength overtake one.

If we take a good look, we will see that we do not need to be compilers of data on the many afflictions destroying people. The number of institutions and wellness centres and hospitals and the media are ready reckoners of the enormity of the predicament we find ourselves in.

We need to examine our lifestyles to see if we can avoid imbalances, and meditation can be very helpful in this regard.

The prerequisite for actively engaging in meditation is a blanking of the mind, making it free of any thoughts. Only the blank white mind screen exists for us to embark on a journey that was practised; we have determined this to be more than five thousand years ago.

Perhaps the meditation we know could only be the scratched surface of what could possibly be much more potent than we could ever imagine. Today and now, meditation is a very powerful medium, once used by the ancient sages or yogis to fine-tune their concentration to a very high level, making them oblivious to everything around them. Who knows? Perhaps it transported them to different realms we may yet come to discover. Possibilities seem endless.

Meditation could possibly be the key to unlock the secrets to ridding the body of all diseases and ailments. It is possible that it can also completely eliminate outside influences and stresses that hinder and impede the smooth running of our bodies.

Through meditation, we can direct and generate concentrated energy to any part of the body to remedy any imbalance in the cells that is causing malfunction or to aid in expelling toxins from the cells before the cells become diseased or perhaps even to eliminate or fix infected cells.

Someday perhaps we may be able to discard some medicines and drugs and painkillers if we can master the art of dispensing concentrated energy to any part of the body that is impaired or in pain or requires any kind of treatment to fix it. Migraine headaches and the like could become things of the past. Perhaps for now we may only know by our personal experiences.

The most important revelation to come out of meditation is that we become more and more who we really are and who we must be, and we gradually realise that we have at last reached a destination that can only end in peace, joy, and happiness.

We know now that, all our lives, prior to the moment we are hit with this reality, we have had a foreign host (or hosts) reside within us that made the true self subservient and condemned us to servitude. This is evident in our daily lives, for as we go about our business, many of us seem like we live in a pseudo world of our own.

Arguments, blame, jealousy, anger, and a retinue of like followers have made their home in our otherwise sacred bodies containing all the elements of the greater universe, deluding us all with the illusion we learned to believe—that they are part and parcel of our lives.

We falsely believe that we will stay so no matter what, and even if one can seek counsel for the eradication of these issues for sanity and reality to prevail, we perpetuate the belief that it is not possible to eliminate or neutralise them completely.

Does this mean we are destined to be unchangeable and it is our lot to suffer? Or do we just prolong our pain by making excuses and not improving our own knowledge and experiences?

In every twist and turn in our lives, when we encounter issues and problems, the ups and downs are recurring lessons. If we have that perception, we will consciously evaluate these stumbling blocks as having some purpose to add to or further our growth and self-worth.

It is as if some magician or sorcerer or wise old man, cunningly, with a devilish grin, more to have fun at our expense in our learning curve, spun a cosmic top that will spin for eternity, setting in motion cycles, millions and billions and more, never ending, never stopping.

Those that are wise and fortunate enough, while pondering on the ingeniousness of such a recurring act, will definitely die wondering about this. How very few of the billions of people on this earth that are forever caught up and enslaved by succumbing to the unintended traps of this cosmic wheel of life and death are aware and wise enough to learn that these traps are self-imposed. Beset with so-called truths that our own imaginations seed.

We watch these seeds take root and grow, as if welcoming pain and wretchedness with open arms. In time, they become our masters by taking over and manipulating our thoughts; we become habitually ingrained with retrograde actions that slowly destroy and devour us.

In our haste to accumulate monetary and material gains, we have given high places to murky and dangerous mind characters, scarred by ego, greed, needs, and wants sitting atop and with love and compassion kicked out the door.

Poverty too has taken a stand; it creeps into the unsuspecting in all societies where means to earn a living may be available but blinds the able-bodied to a life they may inwardly desire.

We should be wary too that when we continuously cry that we are poor or that we badly need money, we will stay poor and get deeper in the trap of needs, as if the universe is only too happy to grant our wishes. Perhaps it is because of this mentality that communities and nations remain disadvantaged through ignorance of the power of our words and thoughts.

Meditation practised carefully and with conviction in the inherent facility of intuition and sensibility will eventually open up, like a secret compartment. Daily meditation will divulge the hidden knowledge that leads to the realisation and self-knowledge that peace and happiness are not only conceivable but attainable so as to speak in this life. It is available anytime, anyplace, whenever we are ready, if ever we recognise and admit to ourselves our superficiality, if we have not already done so.

It is funny and uncanny how we find it so easy to entertain nasty characters that only give us pain and make us uncomfortable, instead of showing them the door out of our mind. We are gradually habitually lumbered not to do so.

To unlearn our habits that demean us, a kind of reverse repetitive action is the ultimate answer. It stands to reason that you backtrack to trace your journey of despair so that you can seek out the source where you first encountered and entertained the demons that have so far maliciously enjoyed their hosting. We can easily overcome and destroy all these ill advisors through a system of meditation carefully worded and imagined on the blank creative canvas, slowly, sturdily, and surely.

When this backward journey commences, then we have acknowledged our dilemma, and we are willing to seek freedom from its hold over us. This newly imbued trust and faith can move mountains in the all-conquering healing powers of meditation.

As we are, we will be ecstatic and most grateful to have encountered and embraced this gift of godlike men of long, long ago, as far back as ancient times of forest dwellers in caves or under trees who have given up all other comforts for most of their lifetimes, their immeasurable sacrifice a boon to us today in a world of high pressures.

A single cell is an entire living entity in itself from a long time ago, before man or animal or trees existed, the power of its will determining its future survival and eventual conception as man. It introduced other multitudes of multicellular creatures millions of years ago.

Billions of cells compose us. Their combined power sustains us. Their multitudes protect us and repair us. They bleed for us; they beat for us. They eat, hear, walk, and see for us. Their service to mankind is incalculable and cannot be measured because they strive to keep us alive any which way they can.

We abuse them in more than a hundred ways. We somehow burn them, drown them, cut them, mutilate them, and destroy them. We invariably ingest toxins with food and with the air we breathe; we fill them with alcoholic drinks and injure them. We even deserted the rich and nutritional natural harvests of the land easily available to us and sought those of laboratories, to add insult to injury. We have mistrusted and abused them with our fractured thoughts.

We have only to visit one hospital to see the casualties of our misdemeanours and injury-inflicting ways, how we punish our cells when all they want to do is protect us, nourish us, and keep us alive.

Yet we apply our ego selves, as we are so taken in by our superficiality and outer happenings and influences, whatever can be used to prop our ego. Hardly any recognition and acknowledgement is given to the splendid work and caring and supporting and fighting that our cells do for us just to keep even this ego self alive.

Cells, hooray! You have a knight and godsend in shining armour from the annals of the past, sent forth from the ancient forest caves and tree shadows to at last make you the centre of attention. Not only to praise you but to give you seconds and minutes and hours and days and weeks and years of unending attention to exercise your will. To empower you to maximise your input for the total well-being and wellness and health of the body you compose.

'Oh, meditation, breathe new life into these much-maligned, long-forgotten charitable and life-saving cells.' In doing this, steadfast and unbending, we absorb the cosmic consciousness to enjoin with our connective being with compassion, without being glued by attachments or with attention—a cosmic generosity of the self.

It is interesting to note that *compassion* contains the primordial sound of the cosmos that was present at the creation of the universe, *om*, as taught by the ancient ascetics. It is said to be the original sound that contains all other sounds, all words, all languages, and all mantras.

Now a whole generation of youth have adapted *oh my god* and turned it into *OMG*. So they too, in a mysterious way, perhaps know om unintentionally and utilise a sound that resonates with creativity.

After a period of relaxation and meditation, we begin to become more aware of who we really are. As in everything, free life flow is of the utmost importance, if not paramount, in anyone's life, without which everything will have no depth but shallowness feigning genuineness. It is a prerequisite for peace and happiness inwardly enjoyed without a show or ostentatiousness—a natural glow without a hint of ego.

When meditation was first practised a long, long time ago, long before the people ventured into India from the Indus Valley, the prime objective was to spread good living and peace amongst all the communities and avoid enmity and conflicts, to dig deep for reasons for friendship and faith in man and God. They believed that if we free the mind of all influences and habits to facilitate clarity and nothingness and just be and open our mind and heart to God, we shall enter God's presence.

To attain this stage, we would imagine that those who embarked on such a journey would have sacrificed all material possessions and comforts to undergo much pain, suffering, penance, and servitude before actually becoming self-realised souls.

Those of us who wish to follow in the paths of holy men and women will have to forgo this life as we know it and withdraw into a world where nothing but divine love and compassion permeate our every thought, without any attachments, and we will have to become oblivious to everyone and everything—a journey that may take more than a lifetime if one ever wavers in their commitment and dedication to reach that state. A lifetime of dedicated selfless service to mankind with a charity of heart and enduring compassion is such a passport too.

Having become proficient in the practice of meditation, the mind becomes a blank screen, on call to manifest any thought with a depth of clarity, like a painting that comes to life with every brush stroke.

The next step is to make that painting jump out of the canvas at will; this ability will provide us with the power to materialise any eventuality, depending on how hungry we are for the force to be with us. Impossible will become possible; dreams will become realities.

All the while, we have to remember that we must have our feet firmly on the ground—we mean really grounded—forever remembering and knowing always that ego and the other bad guys are non-existent in our new-found world; we must remain humble and charitable in all our thoughts, words, and actions, with compassion.

This is the awareness that will always optimise our energy levels, because if for a moment—even for a split second—we let our guard down, hard-earned energy will be sucked out of us, and accordingly, we will lose the power and prowess to aspire in our chosen field of action after we have mastered the art of stilling the mind and preserving every ounce or atom of energy through the great gift we will be able to call on.

Whatever wish we want to manifest in the blank screen, from practice, the easiest way to start, we found, was to just walk and, at the same time, see ourselves walk in front of our physical body, as if we have duplicated ourselves into two walkers. What this does is allow us to project what we wish to achieve or accomplish by watching our double in front of us in that action as if it is happening right now; our projection of the future sees it as a current reality.

This very easy and concentrated technique is very powerful. The desired results are more than likely to be achieved because it is pointedly sharpened and directed with intensity. This is only possible because of our ability to choose our thoughts and remain single-minded and highly focused, disciplined not to waver or allow any other thoughts to have a look-in.

This ensures that we have reached that level of realisation that failure or success is as one, because our detachment has freed us from any ego, needs, or wants. What we thought was not possible in the past is not impossible now. It is now faith that can move mountains.

There have been many instances where we have experienced this phenomenon in play when the mind is fine-tuned to the maximum. What is imagined graphically, in intricate detail and shades and colour, the mind pictures them to be occurring now, because these thoughts cannot be transferred to the future if we have already thought them now.

Prayer is such a medium. When offered with intensity and fervour, it transports one to this place of high energy of goodness and grace. It is a prerequisite of achieving any outcome being embarked on.

That meditation must be undertaken without any desire or need or want or wish for the goal. What we are doing should have feeling or emotion, but it should have no attachment to it but the even, constant thought that the outcome has already occurred. This is of utmost importance because attached emotions are just that, and they tend to consume energy and detract from the actual goal we are working towards.

Be aware that the cosmic wheel spins its own cycle, and we must be in balance and be one with it and not out of it in any way. Any thought or action not in balanced harmony or in violation of its principles will invoke karmic return or failure; we should always remember that cosmic actions and interactions and forces emanating from the cosmic spinning are incredibly mathematically exact and scientifically logical, and perfection cannot be more sublimely whole in every aspect. Any shift or distraction from this perfection will leave us out of it.

It is awe-inspiring to know that our magnificent universe is like a well-oiled colossal machine working for the greater cosmic consciousness, providing all the resources, ever-present and available if used and utilised wisely, and with care mirroring its own compassion and generosity, pulsating with an ever-abundant energy available to all.

Everyone is his or her own universe, all within oneself and evolving within to intensify the energy light within to shine brighter and brighter and brighter and keep the soul and spirit alive long after we dispense of our earthly bodies, perhaps dying yet living forever in the outer dimensions of the universe. If we are sincerely committed in our quest, this will be akin to a shining light showing the way to the ones we meet and greet, to open up their hearts to find their own brightness.

For if we detract from this course and look outside ourselves, we are in danger of sense gratifications absorbing external weaknesses that have a tendency to pollute all our own universes with improper habits that are detrimental to our well-being and what we are meant to do in this life. This externalisation that imbibes these harmful detractions will rob us of the realisation that our life impacts everyone and everything. In this awareness we gain the knowledge that peace and happiness within ourselves will be beneficial for all others too in our lives through the high energy we emit.

If bad-habit-forming or any other influences or known causes of depression and other human frailties that beset us cannot be cured and overcome by conventional and tried and tested means, then meditation has a huge role to play in aiding to restore fervour in one's life by the very nature of its practice.

The technique of meditation through repetition of keywords constantly has the effect of replacing the most hardened of habits that are not conducive to good health and well-being. It is a common practice to chant or repeat with emotion a word or a group of words that resonate with passion, such as mantras or just om, which are supposedly loaded with cosmic power to heal the soul and spirit.

The idea is that just as we grooved a bad habit deeply in our psyche over time by validating illusionary occurrences as real, the opposite effect is achieved when entreatingly chanting with fervour the above mantras or words that we can make up to suit our taste. Om is appropriate and resonates with creativity in its inherent vibration and assists in breathing.

Meditating in this way, with the above empowering mantras or words, achieves the effect of gradually shunting or driving from our mind all these deeply grooved bad habits, to be banished forever, and restores the true self we are born with that is indestructible. Reverting to itself will be the realisation of our place in the scheme of things.

The self, lumbered with fear, self-doubt, low self-esteem, and lack of confidence, accumulating very low vibrations that dim the light within and the soul, weakens during this life and whatever lies beyond the death of the body.

The world may or may not realise it as yet, but by all accounts from the knowledge of the ancient realised souls, every known malady can be overcome if meditation is structured in such a way that the diseased or affected cells of the body can be powerfully energised to rejuvenate them to their original healthy and maximum-functioning states. This knowledge is possibly not widely recorded due to the fact that meditation was largely practised as a means to attract the presence of the divine being; to pay attention to the body would detract from this.

The mind nurtured with creative and uplifting thoughts will grow to embrace life to the fullest, but a mind with debilitating thoughts will make it gravitate to hide away in a dark hole. A mind whose thoughts can be harnessed to still it at will opens up limitless visualisation of potential opportunities for the one that practises this ancient art. We know the often-used 'mind over matter'; what possibilities this phenomenon can open up for mankind is yet to be realised or not widely known.

It is possible the ancients reached such a high state of realisation that they were privy to this power of immense potential, which we cannot even imagine. For instance, if a game of football lasts ninety minutes, the still mind should so be maintained with 100 per cent focus on the match at hand. This means that no distractions at all should disturb the stillness of the mind for ninety minutes.

To be impenetrable to these distractions means that one goes into a detached frame of mind to make this possible. For the detachment to be possible, the act of giving replaces the act of taking, so any selflessness keeps the mind free of any intentions.

The all-important conservation of energy is maintained, for there are no thoughts stealing this much-needed energy which requires fuel to be constantly replenished. When one engages in any activity with a sense of community spiritedness and not of self-interest, sport becomes a beneficial platform for building and upholding stronger and caring societies, with strong family ties extended beyond blood and kin.

When charity of body, mind, and spirit becomes the motivation, it goes a long way in raising families with strong ethics for peaceful and happy coexistence. Young people grow with a sense of purpose and belonging.

All this makes the natural self or the true self, with the intended free-flow life will that is often talked about but is misinterpreted as meaning to do anything one likes, irrespective of the consequences.

Not so, the free-flow will from the very beginning of life on earth when a single-celled organism made its appearance was the will to create to improve itself and outsmart its harsh environment and use all its potential power to survive and grow. We are testament to that.

This same free life will is waiting in everyone to power ahead to unleash its creative power for a better us in particular and a better community in general. This free life will is the creative genius in all of us, and when it is acknowledged that we all possess it, then everything is possible.

Consider all the factors that contribute to sap our energy when we are performing on the field. Apart from these factors, anger and frustration and other negative issues further impede performance.

If we have given careful thought to the disciplines required and the commitment necessary to be an outstanding human being and have made a decision that we have the resolve to give this our best shot, the next step is to look at all the likely images we may conjure to consolidate our one-pointedness towards perfection.

When we now open our eyes to everything and all the happenings in and around us, we find that different perceptions emerge for us to realise how we imagine and will our ways in life.

If we take a closer look at ourselves and all our habits and everything else we do, we will certainly discover a whole new us. How we talk, how we walk, how we eat, how we sleep, what we say, what we do, and whatever else we find about us have concreted through images coinciding with habits adopted; little by little, they became part of us without us realising it.

So everything we do, think, or say will emanate from some need, want, desire, ego, or denial that have come into our psyche, for the most part putting us at risk of some emotional hang-ups that are hard to defeat and destroy, making us prone to all kinds of stresses that weaken us, and even getting us sick.

Now no matter what sport we play or what goal we aspire to, there are many opportunities for advancement if we engage in meditation and adopt the rules for success we have already discussed so far.

We cannot stress the importance of always being our true selves, the self with a soul being enriched constantly by staying connected to the cosmic consciousness, some say to connect with our divinity. Being authentic is being who we are without any pretence, carry-ons, or acting or displaying of denials, needs, wants, or egos. We will know our true selves in this way, the sincere us that is laid bare.

The onset of any medical condition that we were not born with may mean that its acquisition is attributed to this disparity between the true self and the assumed illusory and unreliable self.

If we conjure some images of these inhibitors as identities with an agenda to enter our thoughts and usurp the position of our true selves, then we will see what damage they inflict on the body and the mind. It is as if the mind has a door, and if we forsake our true selves, we open the door for these identities to enter.

Let us take complaining. If we have a tendency to complain, then the false self is at our mind's door, pounding on it for it to be opened. If we succumb to its insistence to gain entry, then it overpowers us, and it will turn us into chronic complainers. Sadly, we will miss all the beauty and wonder of life that is all around us and within us. So could be said of fear and all kinds of phobias and likes and dislikes, love and hate, good and bad, and so many more.

Unfortunately, our short-sightedness has allowed us to entertain a multitude of other ill-advised distractions and to willingly hand the keys to our mind's door. Once entry is gained, then the mind is conquered. They push the true self out of reach of the mind, and then they set about attacking the body.

When these false selves make their home in the mind, the true self is pushed deep down so that its bright light is just a flicker, and the creative willpower is diminished.

These false selves unleash their deadly offsprings—variously named stress, fear, low self-esteem, unhappiness, and demotivation—and attendant woes and illnesses to run riot in our bodies. They are destructive, and the hapless body can only withstand so much. All the cells become weakened, and so do the stretched defence mechanisms, with functionality and production efficiencies hampered to the extent that decay and diseases result.

In this fast-moving world with little time for reflection and relaxation, it is more and more evident that external pressures overwhelm the mind into believing that it is missing out on something. So it creates needs which make people despondent, and mind attachment results.

It seems to be true that nothing material will give lasting satisfaction in life, yet more and more people get caught up in this belief that more will make us satisfied and give us happiness. We want, and the chase for material possessions never stops. If we embark on a quest, because the way we go about it enforces a certain desire, what we want badly we do not often get.

Perhaps answers can only come from within, in a way where we see the outcome as if it had already happened and where we dwell on it constantly, without any desire or want, with a calm and relaxed mind, not with intent, not with ego. Ego could be the doorstopper to our discoveries too.

We are sure that we must have had an experience where we had some sort of issue or problem to resolve, and we tried very hard to do so but to no avail. When we left it alone for a time and got busy doing something else, suddenly out of the blue we figure it out or get some assistance to point to the resolution.

We all know that if we stay relaxed, we are in control of any situation, with a clear head to create appropriate choices. It will indeed be very interesting to know how much more meditation can add to our choices, with a better clarity.

We are in this age of space travel and all things alien, and some of us are beginning to believe that we are being controlled by machines and robots and other sinister forces. There is a great danger that the Internet highway is such a medium that can be unintentionally used to seed belief systems that can dominate the mind to the extent that those of us who are not of strong minds take on mindsets that take over our lives.

We individuals susceptible to these external influences, instead of doing our own research if such topics interest us, take on obsessions that push the true self to the background, and we live that new foreign personality, the true alien and destroyer of our freedom.

We hope that one day soon, scientists and researchers internationally give serious consideration to the use of meditation or at least extensively test how meditation can assist us in attaining good health. If it works in making athletes and sportspeople perform their optimum best, then meditation could do the same for us in other aspects of our lives. Meditation combined with relaxation can hold the key for many other experiences and achievements.

If one tries to focus on any part of the body and repeat mentally and aloud statements such as 'I am feeling that every cell in my body is completely relaxed and healthy, strong and full of vitality', there is a chance that the cells will become that, because they begin to emit that frequency. When we repeatedly perform this sort of mantra, in time we may find that that part of the body we concentrate on or focus our words on will possibly heal.

Relaxation and meditation should become our accessory at all times or whenever possible, without losing the presence of whatever we are doing. It will be a matter of time before we will become adept at relaxing our whole body from toes to head on call; mere recall of the thought of meditation will relax us immediately. When we give ourselves some keywords to trigger the desired reactions, relaxation is made easier.

Meditation and relaxation should be incorporated in all schools universally.

Perhaps someday humanity will awake from its deep slumber, and it will explore pure freedom through relaxation and meditation. A focus on the true self and the possibilities for healing both the body and mind and other outcomes can be monumental for human advancement.

Imagine a world where people walk around with free and nonprogrammed minds and choices resonating with true being, no longer battered and bruised by any sort of advertising and marketing ingenuity of hard sell. We will at last feel and know that our choices are not put into our minds, ears, nose, skin, and eyes but come from a purposeful intent all our own—no more impulse buying or being taken in by all kinds of sales pitches and gimmicks.

What a difference this will make to our hip pocket and, more importantly, to our physical and mental health, because competition will take on a new meaning; growers, producers, suppliers, wholesalers, and retailers will be constantly improving the quality and benefits of their merchandise if they are to survive in the marketplace. Only those that are totally committed and sincere in their services will succeed, and for all others, their advertising dollar will have lost its power and hold over people forever.

At last, people power will rule, with compounding benefits in well-being and health. Healthy minds and healthy bodies mean a diminishing drain on healthcare resources and families and carers.

When people are in touch with their real selves, a calming peace descends on them that will ultimately make them more caring and compassionate and charitable. Could it be that when we get in touch with our true self, we inevitably reach a divinity we strangely fear to admit and acknowledge as so?

This fear of loss of everyday pleasures is unfounded because it does not aim to take away all our everyday pleasures but enhances them to make our lives more meaningful and purposeful, deep and not vain. This knowledge that is realised overwhelmingly takes us to the path of compassion, which is in the universal cosmic consciousness.

Love cannot be feigned any more because it is an expression of selflessness and not selfishness. Men and women will find life more exciting and live each new day with a rejuvenated enthusiasm. Trust and honesty and wholesome living and lifestyles will mean disruptions will be taken as a matter of course and will be readily flipped and seen as opportunities to advance further. Divorce may not eventuate because first impressions will be lasting impressions.

At last, we will open our eyes wide, and when we look, we will really see the wonder of this life that greets us at every turn, no longer blinded by our own needs and wants and ego. We will know the footpath we walk on and admire the beauty and nature all around us.

Now we will walk straight, with a smile on our faces and with the knowledge that the world is at our feet; we will all be oozing with confidence and facing every challenge head-on.

No more of that slouch, no more of that strained face, no more of that aloofness, no more of that ego, no more of that false self—only the beautiful real people we were meant to be. Ugliness will not exist any more; gone will be those eyes of the false self. When we are not relaxed, our faces can betray what we feel or what we are going through; the way we walk and the way we talk betray us too.

This realisation that reaches us can only be in our best interest, for what we elevate to touches everyone. Not to consider the universe and its workings purposeful is the greatest mistake we can make and will do ourselves and the whole world much harm.

How so? The moment we find fault, the moment we lie, the moment we commit any selfish and uncharitable act, the moment we speak ill, the moment we complain, know then and there that we have unearthed a flaw in ourselves. Left unchecked, it will slowly but surely consume us. We have expressed in that dark moment a deep need or want unquenched.

This realisation is our very welcome saviour, for from this day, we start our therapy of acceptance by bringing it out to dissipate. It is our release from a great burden carried for so long, perhaps from before our entrance into this earth.

We are all as universes within universes, and each of us function the same. We live in our own universe, which is all of us, including our bodies, mind and soul and spirit, a microcosm of the greater universe. We imitate the universe as we own it, and the way we treat our universe is a reflection on the greater universe. We are constituted by the same materials and elements, and we react accordingly. Being so, could it be that we also create our own willed disasters unleashed by nature?

Astrology also has a role to play. Vast studies have shown that we are affected by planetary and other heavenly bodies that frolic in the solar system. We know in a similar way the moon affects the tides and helps farmers too of when to put seed to ground.

Now astrological predictions are useful in that they bring awareness to us that we are constantly faced with challenges at the whim of the outer world. If we keep our sense of perspective and apply common sense, we will be all the wiser to ride out the pitfalls we face.

Quite often, the deep need in us brings to the fore anger and bitterness, which tend to harm us. Meditation will make this dissipate and never come back, because our true self knows not of it. Meditation is the answer to enduring happiness in all relationships, including marriage.

If we look beyond our own universe, we get caught up in all the other universes around us, and we take their vibrations, which may impede what our wishes and dreams are. True to form, they may remain only as wishes and dreams, because we look externally; all the difficulties associated with our quests cloud our clarity of thoughts, which may make us withdraw the chase and even make us introverted.

In this modern day of great technological advancements, with resources in abundance and money easily accumulated through charitable organisations and communities, research by dedicated scientists to find cures for incurable diseases, including the many cancers, is at a feverish pace. Meanwhile, immeasurable pain and suffering overwhelm whole families and carers to no end when someone in the family is affected by these scourges and causers of miseries.

Even though there are reports of people overcoming many of these curses of mankind through various regimes other than only conventional chemotherapy and other medical aids, we seem to be blind to them.

Besides these reports, there are scores of books on alternative ways to treat many so-called incurable diseases, but they are largely and alarmingly ignored. Sadly, many people miss out on all this knowledge, as all are not well informed or even biased enough to at least have a chance of trying something different.

In spite of this, whole generations of sick people too are not privy to or encouraged to try whatever disciplines are proven to be effective to regain their once healthy and disease-free celled bodies where conventional medicine unfortunately has been unable to help them.

We have at our disposal various diets and foods that are both nutritional and disease fighting, but many opt for the easier option of pills and drugs. Vegetarian diets and organic foods are spoken of as disease fighting too. Exercises and various physical activities also seem to help.

Then there are others who believe diseases can be healed with a lengthy period of continuous days and nights spent solely with concentrated doses of specific foods or juices or nutrients selected for their known usefulness in destroying unhealthy, diseased cells.

Excessive laughter brought about by continuous viewing of comedies is also suggested. Perhaps we could discover 'laughter is the best medicine' to be more than mere words.

It has been proven that engaging in social activities, such as listening to music, singing, dancing, and engaging in sports and games, are of great health benefit too.

Then there are relaxation and meditation techniques that have come into their own as very effective against all ailments that torture the body. And then there are the various yoga practices. Up to this point in time, the true depth of the effects of the relaxation and meditation combination has somehow been overlooked, perhaps because of the assumed spiritual, religious, or Eastern origins of meditation.

Decades into the future, when alien greed and self-interests and other associated ills are realised for what they are and shunned, humanity as a whole would have turned the corner and will perceive past desecrations and inglorious actions that lowered the vibrations of the human race for so long and stifled consciousness as unfortunate necessary lessons.

Amongst them will be those who sadly perpetrate myths of their ego—those that are unwittingly caught up and indoctrinated through years of externally centred and focused knowledge and education, very one-sided and limiting. Subsequently the more fulfilling and permanent aspects of the innermost dimension are usually dismissed or ignored.

It is an irony that academic education, for a large part, has created a buffer against openness to entertain all ideas that seek to lift humanity. It is possible that important discoveries could be staring in the faces of researchers and scientists, but because of their misplaced ideological belief in logic and facts, they have missed the boat in not taking a holistic approach by taking a chance on intuition and mystery. The great Einstein indirectly alluded to this when he concluded that mystery is a challenge.

Hearsay is never given a chance, for cold reasoning stored in volumes of text gives credence to many follies and falsity. False selves spinning yarns in the guise of the loophole of lobbying has become a pastime, parading in disguised garments with political favours and cronyism. We rightfully believe that seasoned and experienced people that serve all institutions with all their knowledge and expertise in their fields of employment ably manage their areas of control. We now know why many don't.

We have made great, giant strides in various and difficult endeavours and marvel at our discoveries, but we wonder and ask ourselves how we constantly and hopelessly fail in successfully executing tangible and measured outcomes. Perhaps selves that have forsaken their inner judgement of honour through delusions of grandeur forsake their true selves for their own ends.

A long, long time ago, when man made his first appearance on earth with a strong will to survive and a strong will to feed and protect his family no matter what the odds, he persevered to overcome inactivity and its attendants to keep his creativity alive. He needed no relaxation and meditation because of his fighting spirit and single-mindedness; communities existed with righteousness and disciplines that upheld them, with no distractions that dulled the will.

Then as time went by, despondency resulted in the will of action decreasing because of easily acquired material and financial gains and an environment of excesses and greed. As was recorded in the Gita, through despondency and attachment, when man descended to a new low, Hare Krishna made his appearance on earth and revealed how we can overcome all our troubles and resultant weakened wills and confusion of false selves with the true self.

For in relaxation and meditation, there lies the compelling rejuvenation of the long-lost free life will, the foundation of life in its ability, if practised wisely, to empower the mind and body to energise the true self to lead to the knowledge and ultimate realisation of who we really are. Our search for the truth will always lead us to ourselves.

Just compare what is within our head and our body and limbs and what lies outside us. If our bodies and senses can withstand us being paralytic, imbibing alcohol, influencing our minds with different drug concoctions, or gluttony and are none the worse for wear, there must be compelling reasons that deep down within us lies a well of untapped knowledge.

If meditation is so invaluable and potent for our prolonged well-being, it must be considered that there is no permanency in what our genes data tell us at any given time. Possibilities are that complete transformations are taking place all the time, and when the art of meditation is mastered, we will know that we could have foolishly fallen prey to the delusional impermanency of being attached to the outside happenings and possessions.

The power of the body and imagination and imaging is yet to be tapped fully and could hold the answer to all of life's demands and problems. Part of that is the suggestion of tapping intuitions whereby we imagine that there is a huge reservoir of answers and solutions. All we have to do is turn the flow on, and it should pour out the knowledge we require for our creativity.

Brainstorming is known for its effectiveness. We are certain that if we recall when we first had an idea of what we set out to achieve and the intensity of that quest and if we achieved it, we will now know what part our subconscious played in it.

Likewise, we must be wary of what vibrations we project by our actions, our speech, and our thoughts if we are struggling to let go of them. Our subconscious mind is ever eager to manifest that which we propagate and harvest as if we desire that to happen to us. If we think that we need to lose weight for health reasons but keep repeating that it is impossible to lose weight and that we will not get better, our subconscious mind works to that end. We will not lose weight, and we will stay sick.

Now we know what impact relaxation and meditation has in anyone's life. Knowing this and having a great knowledge of the workings of the subconscious and conscious minds and how our body functions and what it needs to stay healthy, the ancient seers understood life and its complexities and ups and downs; they left this gift of meditation to posterity, at last unearthed.

To live life to the fullest and enjoy the fruits of this life and not hold back or have any regrets, all we have to do is see this happening right now. The three keys to what we really wish for and set to fruition is meditation, relaxation, and imagination. If these became part of our everyday life, every second of the day, then our life will become glorious and precious. Our charity will show no bounds, and we will see beauty in everyone and everything; we will be in constant ecstasy.

When we reach this balance in our lives, nothing will dampen our spirits, for we are in touch with the cosmic consciousness.

Before we acquire this knowledge of the three keys and become aware of their relevance in our lives, perhaps we have some needs that preoccupy us. We must get to the bottom of these needs to enable us to dissipate them through appropriate actions.

We keep at it and keep at it, not wishing or dreaming—just being in it. This is the mystery of our lives that we cannot explain, but it is proven time after time that our will has a way, with stubborn determination; perhaps it is through a state of being. Many lives are testament to it due to their sheer will to succeed.

In everything we say, in everything we do, and in everything we think, we must not let any doubt or weariness or negativity dare intrude, because they all have a tendency to set us back. Instead, in everything we say, say it with love and goodness and charity of the heart. In everything we do, do it with love and with goodness and charity of the heart. So too in everything we think; we must think with love and goodness and charity of the heart.

If we wish to achieve anything, see it as if it has already happened. If we want jobs, we see ourselves in the jobs. If we want a particular car, we see ourselves driving that car. If we want a new suit, we see ourselves in the new suit. No matter what we want, we should see ourselves already with it.

Two forces are at play here: We have a thought of some event happening in the not-too-distant future. What our thought has done is bring the future to the moment we had the thought. Then what our subconscious mind does is, it takes that cue and says, 'Right, I am now tailoring everything to suit to bring it to the now.'

When we are out and about, we at last know that our every step and every move and every thought are immersed in loving and adoring and appreciating everything. This love is from the depth of creation; it connects us and makes us one with the whole world, for our eyes are only for love.

Whenever we feel a little down, before the onset of any negative thoughts, we let our imagination emerge as a martial artist, with swift lightning moves that obliterate them—sometimes karate, sometimes kung fu, even with a sword and nunchucks. No more will they dare tempt and delude us.

Love is living itself; if every cell of our body reverberates with it, then it becomes a strong bonding foundation. When it is expressed with that warmth from the core of the heart, then it has a strong effect and influence upon all. The power of love is enduring, and if it is given with hugs and cuddles, its effect will melt the coldest hearts. Every parent has this opportunity to empower and strengthen their children with this love.

Meditation is a natural state of living; over time, we have forgotten that it is just to be. As simple as that.

Our lifestyles these days make continually being in a relaxed state almost impossible. So here's the simple solution. The same principle applies, as it does in electricity. When we are not relaxed, we have increased the resistance against the free flow of energy. It is similar to the current trying to make its way to the light bulb when the power switch is switched on.

For the desired brightness, the copper tubes are proportionally configured to do that for maximum efficiency. In our case, the stresses we impose on ourselves under different circumstances fail to circumvent the satisfactory powering of our cells. The energy within us is not enough to feed the trillions of cellular helpers in our material make-up. In time, we feel the impact of this deficiency in many ways.

There is an easy fix that just needs an awareness that a well-maintained engine can provide horsepower for us to perform many activities without much effort. When faced with any issues, the simple rule of thumb is to turn to the inner I and at the same time breathe easily. As this is given a conscious effort, gradually we get used to the idea that oxygen is reaching all the parts of our body, as if by our call to do so. While the focus is directed within us, it may help to imagine or visualise that all the cells of our bodies from the head to the feet are slowly receiving all the nourishment through the air we are breathing.

Eventually, the R factor pressure loses its effect, as we have no thoughts or ignore its existence as we become more energetic to soldier on with our activities. The dynamics of this easy lifestyle lies in its act of blocking out all outside disturbances, distractions, and influences, with an inside focus.

It is a great way for sportspeople to hone their skills in their chosen code, because there is no leakage of any vitality through useless attention seeking driven by our ego.

CHAPTER 16

RELAXATION

A prerequisite to meditation is relaxation.

Oxygen is our life force; therefore, rhythmically breathing in and out slowly through the nostrils is very important in all activities. Loose clothes are recommended so as not to interfere with our concentration. Initially, a quiet time and place is ideal to block out as much noise and interference as possible. Early morning is best.

After we have had a restful and sufficient amount of sleep so as not to fall asleep during this session of relaxation, we may commence.

We will adopt the sleeping position where we lie straight on our backs with our arms and legs extended away from the head. The reason we do this is to have no physical pressure on any part of our body, as would happen if we adopt sitting or squatting or any other position.

We breathe slowly in and out through the nostrils during the entire relaxation session. We keep our eyes open and point them to the direction of the toes, and if we cannot actually see our toes, we imagine them. Then we very slowly move our eyesight towards the feet and ankles, towards the knees and thighs and lower body and stomach and waist, and towards the arms and neck and chin and mouth and nose and eyes and ears and head. We then close our eyes and recall the steps our eyes followed from toes to head.

Now we open our eyes and begin moving our sight from our heads and ears and eyes and nose and mouth and chin and neck and arms towards our waist and stomach and lower body and thighs and towards our knees and ankles and feet and toes. Now we close our eyes and recall the steps our eyes followed from head to toes.

What we have done in the above steps was acclimatise ourselves to our body form and make us aware of our whole body from toes to head. If we cannot avoid interfering thoughts, we shall persevere to get used to the above steps, as we will learn how to still our minds later.

Now we will keep our eyes open and introduce a few words to assist us with relaxing every cell in our body. We begin again with our eyes, or mind's eye, set on the toes, and we simultaneously repeat 'I am feeling that every cell in my toes is completely relaxed'. As we move our gaze towards our heads, we replace *toes* with the other parts in the above sequence practised.

We repeat the process, now starting with the head across all the other parts to the toes, repeating 'I am feeling that every cell in my head is completely relaxed' and replacing *head* with the part we are moving through.

Now with our eyes closed, we proceed with the reverse of the above, repeating 'I am feeling that every cell in my toes is completely relaxed', repeating the above, with *toes* being replaced with the next part passed until we reach our heads.

Practice makes perfect; this holds true if we make the effort to spend these treasured moments, for if we do this, our cells will thank us for maintaining a healthy body. When we believe we have done that, we move to the next stage.

Still in the prone floor position, we attempt to create a double of ourselves. This double will rise and face us, standing upright at our feet. This duplicate of us will scan us lying at its feet from our toes to our heads and from our heads to our toes. All the while, we are repeating 'I am feeling that every cell in my toes is completely relaxed', replacing *toes* with the part we are passing through.

We have found that if we do this by creating an energy body outside us, relaxation becomes more pronounced. In time, this practice will enable us to be in relaxation mode 24/7 just by constantly recalling our created energy duplicate, which sees us as always relaxed. A kind of automated relaxation mode comes to being.

Now that we know how to effectively relax, we can take relaxation to the next step. We know we are composed of millions of cells grouped throughout our body to form parts and organs that perform specific tasks for the total functioning of the human species. We suggest that we brush up on our study of the human body to enable us to target specific groupings or cells forming that part.

As an example, if we wish to focus on the blood vessels and the blood that flows through them, we begin to picture our whole body and our duplicate looking through us and tracking all the blood vessels and capillaries that traverse, at first starting with the toes and moving upwards towards the head in the sequence we have practised. All the while, we are repeating 'I am feeling that every cell in my blood and blood vessels is completely relaxed'. We repeat this as many times as we wish, not forgetting to start again from the head downwards and ending at the toes.

It is an amazing world that we can experience if we become adept at this instant relaxation technique. We will be able to take on any form, such as a miniature of ourselves, and explore any part of our body by simply imagining that we are on a journey of discovery and see up close any area of the body we wish. We can enter through a pore in one of our fingers and roam throughout the interior of our bodies and hitch a ride in our flowing blood or be rocked within our beating heart or sprayed by digestive juices.

When we begin to experience this on call, then we know that we have mastered relaxation for the overwhelming benefits it can provide for our ongoing well-being.

We are now ready for the next step—stilling the mind.

Chapter 17

STILLING THE MIND

If we have not engaged in this previously, we will find that it is quite difficult to harness all our thoughts in a single sitting. This next exercise will be experienced with the automated relaxation mode we just mastered.

We shall keep the same lying position we used when we practised relaxation and the same conditions for total concentration. Just to remind us: we must have loose clothes and a quiet place away from too much noise to start us off.

Oxygen is our life force; therefore, rhythmically breathing in and out slowly through the nostrils is very important in all activities, including stilling the mind. We shall move our total concentration to a spot which is midway between our eyes, above the eyeline on our forehead, as if we are looking at the end of our nose. With eyes closed, we picture a white blank screen.

If we are doing this for the first time, fluttering thoughts will be hard to contain, but our persistence will endure. We can do this by letting the thoughts occur and gradually decrease. Eventually, when we are able to keep out all thoughts, we will only see a white blank screen.

We hold on to this, what we see, and without any pressure, gradually we will reach a state where all we see will be a white blank screen enveloping us with a stillness—'thoughtlessness'. We will be in a totally relaxed state.

Finally, we are ready to embark on our meditation journey that will take us towards freedom.

Chapter 18

MEDITATION

We have established ourselves in both relaxation and stilling the mind. We now are ready to embark on a journey that will lead to eventual self-realisation.

The most important step is to face up to all our illusory false selves, which have for so long kept us from knowing our true authentic selves. This we know because at different times, these false selves turned out in different disguises, such as ego, needs, and wants.

We can disguise them, but we cannot hide their intent that displays at different times and in different individuals—anger, ego, denial, anxiety, fear, low self-esteem, phobias, and a host of other offshoots, like jealousy, envy, complaints, and dissatisfaction with life. We may have many reasons for having these absorbed into us, but it is now time to dump them and our attachments that make us despondent.

We will still stick to the same prone position in which we practised relaxation and try to remain in the automated relaxed state. With our double standing at our feet, watching us, we shall fix our gaze on the white blank screen and repeat these words: 'I am feeling that every cell in my body is completely relaxed, and my creative free will reinforces my true authentic self'.

Oxygen is our life force; therefore, rhythmically breathing in and out slowly through the nostrils is very important in all activities, including meditation. After repeating the above in a session of about at least thirty minutes, we now reflect on how we conduct ourselves outside the meditation room.

For meditation to be effective, we now take the next step of becoming acutely aware of all our thoughts, words, actions, and deeds in our daily lives. These now only propagate high values with a giving kind of attitude that displays charity and compassion of the heart. No more denials, no more regrets, no more dissatisfaction, no more envy, no more jealousy, no more complaints, no more attachments, no more anger, no more hate, and no more of anything that lowers our mood and dampens our spirits and destroys sweet life.

If we persist in stubborn determination, we will eventually come to realise that at last our road towards freedom has been reached. With the gradual shedding of the baggage that held us back, we are equipped with a new perception of participation and upliftment. A new beginning opens up a whole new world of peace and happiness that we did not believe possible.

We are now in a powered relaxed state. We are now able to blank our minds to have no thoughts or call at will any thought. Most importantly, we are now who we really are, our self-realised authentic selves, bursting with pure energy to power our creative wills for the common good.

Breathing is very important at all times. Another very effective breathing exercise is to place your right hand firmly on your stomach, around your navel, and breathe out through your nostrils as many times as you wish. It will be good if you can do it about twenty-five times. You will feel your stomach go in, and your chest pushes out. This helps bring you to yourself, as your attention is brought to your body and away from your mind.

With introspective examination, we unearth our genius for all possibilities to propel ourselves to the highest aspect of our consciousness.

CHAPTER 19

THE HEAVEN ABOVE

There is no logical way to the discovery of these elemental laws. There is only the feeling of intuition, which is helped by a feeling for the order lying behind the appearance.

Albert Einstein

As above, so below.

If the solar system is the great power generator of our universe, then the earthling is the microcosm of it in the way the IR relationship operates. This chapter is to demonstrate that all calculations in the below occurrences in our galaxy all reduce to the number 9.

In my research on the number 9 I came across a video called Tides of Time posted by Mahabharat (published on Mar 31, 2018), subtitled Mahabharat by Sadhguru, Yugas – Tides of Time:

The Bhagavata is one of Hinduism's eighteen great puranas or histories composed in Sanskrit and promotes that we tune in to the synchronicity of the great geometry of the universe.

We go through four periods or age cycles in the earth's evolution according to the functioning of the planets with respect to the sun.

These are the tides of time that we must tune into according to the rules of life so that we do not spin out of control.

We play games with time as we are born and ruled by time.

The first is Satya Yuga which lasts 5184 years, then Treta Yuga for a period of 3888 years followed by Dvapura Yuga of 2592 years and then Kali Yuga which is for 1296 years.

The next half continues with Kali Yuga for 1296 years, then Dvapura Yuga, 2592 years, then Treta Yuga for 3888 years and then back to Satya Yuga for another 5184 years.

All the Yugas complete a cycle which lasts 25920 years.

It takes 25920 years to form a circle by the orbit of our solar system to go around the super sun.

25920 divided by the 60 heart beats = 432.

60 heart beats a minutes × 60 minutes = 3600 times.

3600 × 24 hrs = 864000 / 2 = 432000.

A healthy person takes 15 breaths per minute and 21600 breaths in a 24 hour period.

15 breaths × 60 minutes = 900 per hour, 900 × 24hrs = 21600.

1 nautical mile = 1 degree which is 60 minutes and 360 minutes × 60 minutes = 21600 nautical miles at the equator.

The earth's one orbit round the Sun is made up of 27 sections each with 4 subsections with 108 subsections in the complete orbit.

Diameter of Sun × 108 = distance between sun and earth.

Diameter of moon × 108 = distance between moon and earth.

It is interesting to note that the English or French *kilometre* adds up to 108 in its numeric value.

As a result of the above 108 is a significant number for meditation, prayers and chanting in Hinduism. Malas or garlands of beads are usually made with 18, 27, 54 or 108 beads.

108 is also an important number in Buddhism and Jainism.

This is also so in some Tibetan, Chinese, Christian, Moslem and Tibetan cultures.

From the above, you will notice that all the calculations reduce to 9.

CHAPTER 20

THE OMNIPRESENT 9

If you only knew the magnificence of the 3, 6 and 9,
you would have the key to the Universe.

Nikola Tesla

Here we are going to discover the most mystical and fascinating number that has immense power over all life. Understanding the power of 9 can unlock the almighty and intriguing play of the universe in its many guises.

We shall start with circles or spheres, such as the sun, moon, and earth. The first thing that comes to mind is that they all have 360 degrees.

Our birthdates also consist of three circles, each representing approximately a third of our total life span on earth. The first one is the reduced number of the month of our birth, the second is the reduced number of our day of birth, and the third is the reduced number of our year of birth. Here too, all are in the vicinity of 360 degrees and could be an indication of how centred we are through all the dramas that we enact and experience from birth to death.

Within us too is a genuine connection to the sun through the fire element that provides our regulatory body temperature. Our shared life force with every breath we take is the air element, which miraculously sustains us through the divine oxygen and the carbons we breathe to sustain plant life. Then there are the numerous elements we take in through our food that provide specific electrical charges when they interact with chemicals in our body.

Our eyes too are divinely imbued by their shapes and as a link between our outer and inner worlds, like two triangles joined at the base. The electrical current that powers our outside world in its flow and resistance factors corresponds with our behaviours.

We will soon see that our mode of communication through spoken and written English is coded spiritually.

CHAPTER 21

THE CODE

I am in physics for I am an electrician, a mathematician and in the geometry of the engine. And in Panini too.

Devad

What one man calls God, another calls the laws of physics.

Nikola Tesla

M_y fascination for the independent and stand-alone characteristics of the number 9 led me to unearth a whole new way of looking at our lives. Through further research, I have found that there is no doubt that whoever was the architect of our mathematics and language was indeed a genius.

This led me to Panini, a grammarian of India and a master craftsman of numbers and alphabets, who lived sometime between the fourth and the seventh century BC.

His exceptional intelligence and innovative expertise resulted in organising the interplay of letters and numbers in a very highly complex and systematic arrangement in scripting Sanskrit.

Panini is also regarded as likely to have contributed to the formation of the binary computer code for the way he enriched the Sanskrit language.

Chapter 22

SANSKRIT

COMPLETE OR PERFECT

Panini's grammar has been evaluated from various points of view. After all these different evaluations, I think that the grammar merits asserting—that it is one of the greatest monuments of human intelligence.

G. G. Joseph

The arrangements of letters in Sanskrit are referred to as the garland of letters, likened to a mala often used in meditation.

Devanagari (heavenly/sacred script of the city) is one of a type of scripts used for writing down Sanskrit texts in India, and *Deva* means 'heavenly'. It is important to note that 'the order of the letters is based on articulatory phonetics'. This influenced Sanskrit as a 'divinely sophisticated medium for communication'. This must be the reason why Sanskrit is called the language of the gods.

Sanskrit uses 'simple versatile building blocks called Dhatu, a set of 2012 root words, from which words of an entire language are derived'. All words are derived from these root words; no names of objects are given, only the possibility of forming any number of objects and things. This means that the 2012 root words are fixed for eternity, but creation of new words is based on the attributes and properties of these roots.

We will soon discover the English language's link to Sanskrit through the given number values to each alphabet. By virtue of this, English is so ingeniously structured too, to show our connectivity to the divine.

Chapter 23

THE EVOLUTION OF THE ENGLISH ALPHABET

The intellectual debt of Europe to Sanskrit literature has thus been undeniably great; it may perhaps become greater in the years to come.

Arthur Anthony Macdonell
(1900)

The ingenious method of expressing every possible number using a set of ten symbols (each symbol having a place value and an absolute value) emerged in India. The idea seems so simple nowadays that its significance and profound importance is no longer appreciated. Its simplicity lies in the way it facilitated calculation and placed arithmetic amongst useful inventions. The importance of this invention is more readily appreciated when considered that is way beyond the two greatest men of Antiquity, Archimedes and Apollonius.

Pierre-Simon Laplace (1749–1827)

Archimedes was a Greek mathematician, physicist, engineer, inventor, and astronomer, born circa 287 BC. Apollonius was a Greek mathematician (geometer) and astronomer, born between late third and early second centuries BC.

This is an observation in 1786 by Sir William Jones (1746–1794) of Sanskrit's influence on the English language:

> The Sanskrit language, whatever be its antiquity, is of a wonderful structure; more perfect than the Greek, more copious than the Latin, and more exquisitely refined than either, yet bearing to both of them a stronger affinity, both in the roots of verbs and the forms of grammar, than could not possibly have been produced by accident; so strong indeed, that no philologer could examine them all three, without believing them to have sprung from a common source, which, perhaps, no longer exists: there is a similar reason, though not quite so forcible, for supposing that both the Gothic and the Celtic, though blended with a very different idiom, had the same origin with the Sanskrit, and the old Persian might be added to this family, if this were the place for discussing any question concerning the antiquities of Persia.

Panini, as mentioned earlier, was the Sanskrit grammarian born in Shalatula, a town on the Indus River in present-day Pakistan. He was a genius of India whose innovation in systemising the Sanskrit grammar to make it an all-encompassing package for communication was ingenious.

Panini makes reference to his predecessor, a grammarian, Sphotayana, who was the originator of the concept Sphota, meaning 'bursting, opening' and 'spurt' in Sanskrit. In all likelihood, the idea was to formulate the spoken language as a vehicle to express more than what the words mean by their dictionary definitions.

Now we know that our connectivity to the cosmos through our communications in all vibratory frequencies is measured by the letter values. Our very emotions and thoughts coded in the words are revealed through their numerical value. This is evident in those words that reduce to 9, which align with the idea of the divine. Even Panini's name does.

Through the Sanskrit language rose the algebraic nature of using letters to represent relationships between unspecified numbers in the field of mathematics in India. By representing numbers with words, the modern number system emerged as a link through the structure of language.

It is astonishing that mathematics then, almost 2500 years ago, evolved through the development of language systems in India. It is a question that can be answered by looking at some significant words that emerge from the numbers that are assigned to all the alphabets.

Could it be possible that Panini, and possibly Sphotayana before him, looked at the heavens and their relationship to humans mathematically? Is this is how he decided the order of both the numbers and alphabets?

Evidence suggests that using the number values at first to come up with words closely aligned to the divine was his first inspiration. From this point, his genius finally gave us the English we know and use today.

Examples are *I*, *R*, *sun*, *ego*, *source*, *love*, *lover*, and *eyes*, whose numerical equivalents all add up to or are reduced to the number 9.

Chapter 24

GAME OF I'S

Who is that loves and who that suffers? He alone
stages a play with himself, who exists save him?

Sri Anandamayi Ma
(30th April1896 –27thAugust 1982)

The origin of *I* comes from the Latin word *ego*. The *I* is most
often the symbol for electrical current.

To know the true I, we must acknowledge that there is another I in
all of us that causes us much grief most of the time. This I, known as
the superego, sprouts its own version through reactionary tendencies
of the senses. The subject identifies with the object and loses itself in
the object; the observer takes the identity of the observed. The ego (I)
fluctuates back and forth through id and superego, like a game of I's.

How do we come to accept that we are all two I's in one? What we
know is embraced in our physicality and body and sense interactions,
bound by time and limitations. The one we don't know is timeless
and limitless.

I is the formless aspect that is in the spiritual or divine eternity—
that which exists in permanence when we discard our bodies.

In my view, if we experience prolonged suffering and pain, it
means our spirit ego has been usurped by our sense ego. Or we are
suppressing our spirit ego.

The I that has acquired a name soon after birth henceforth set
about believing this identification with the body. When our names
are praised, we exult in confidence, but all hell breaks loose when

our names are sullied. We become so much our names that we are ultimately attached to our projections, to such an extent that our thoughts continually hijack us. Reactions unsettle us and result in a pendulum of high and low moods and feelings. It is like a puppeteer that remote-controls our lives.

There is a force within us that wishes to continually break free; that is why we suffer much unpleasantness. The one I is self-esteemed, and the other takes a mantle of self-importance and thrives in self-ignorance.

CHAPTER 25

PATH TO 9

Call it a bird, an insect, an animal or a man, call it by
any name you please, one serves one's own self in every
one of them.

Sri Anandamayi Ma
(30th April 1896–27th August 1982)

For almost my entire adulthood, the meaning of my life was
something that was desperately sought. My digging into the depths
of all resources has finally made me turn inwards to look deep within
myself.

After hours and hours of reflective meditation, there is a peace
in me now, with the discovery of the divine. An innermost urge to
share what has come to be is this story, the surprising discovery of my
fervent passion. Life has a way to satisfy our deepest desires, provided
there is a persistence to persevere with unfailing willingness.

My fascination with the number 9 began after coming across
3, 6, 9, and 18 in the Gita. With constant reflection on the reason
for the eighteen chapters, my attention was drawn to an article on
Nikola Tesla and his take on 3, 6, and 9. This stirred something
within me to pursue these numbers further to unearth a coding that
really excites me.

CHAPTER 26

ALPHABETS AND NUMERALS

If you knew the magnificence of the three, six and nine, you should have a key to the Universe.

Nikola Tesla

The English alphabet letters *A* to *Z* are represented by the numbers, consequently 1 to 9, 1 to 9, and 1 to 8:

A, J, S   = 1
B, K, T   = 2
C, L, U   = 3
D, M, V   = 4
E, N, W   = 5
F, O, X   = 6
G, P, Y   = 7
H, Q, Z   = 8
I, R   = 9

CHAPTER 27

THE ELECTRICIAN

The intuitive mind is a sacred gift and the rational mind is a faithful servant. We have created a society that honours the servant and has forgotten the gift.

Albert Einstein

The magnificent sun is the largest sphere in our solar system, providing us with light and heat. It's revered as a deity by a multitude of cultures throughout the world. It is in the rays and also in our electricity.

CHAPTER 28

FLOW AND RESISTANCE

> If you wish to understand the Universe, think of energy, frequency and vibration.

> Nikola Tesla

In Ohm's law for electric current, E stands for voltage, I stands for current (amps), and R stands for resistance.

In 1827, Georg Simon Ohm, a German physicist, published his treatise on what we know today as Ohm's law in electricity.

If we take the sun or source of the universe as the electrician, the human drama is played out in a similar manner: the resistance (ohm), the conductance (mho), and the 'photoconductivity' of us in either accepting or rejecting the knowledge of the truth of ourselves. The greater the light of love that shines in our lives, the less pain and suffering we endure.

It is not a coincidence that electricity is in our normal body temperature, as the fire element, at 36.9 degrees Celsius.

CHAPTER 29

NIKOLA TESLA

18

Nikola Tesla (10 July 1856–7 January 1943) was a genius who was both an inventor and an engineer. He gifted the world with the alternating current (AC) electric system, Tesla coil, for radio technology, amongst other creations.

Nikola phonetically equates to the reduced number 9, same as *inventor, electrician, magnetic wheels, transmissions, tower, communicate, signals,* and *spaces*.

Perhaps his use of eighteen napkins to clean cutlery had something to do with the above.

Chapter 30

EGO IGNORANCE

> There are only two ways to live your life. One is
> as though nothing is a miracle. The other is as though
> everything is a miracle.

> Albert Einstein

Our eyes are our organs of sensory sight, the visual gateway to the outside material world. Our focal point of view is triangular, 180 degrees. The view if we look inwards is also three angled, 180 degrees. Inside and outside views enclose 360 degrees of sight.

If you consider the meaning of *holistic* in philosophy, it comprises the whole of our existence, inside and outside. This suggests that if we ignore or neglect our spiritual side, we shall be out of balance and in strife.

CHAPTER 31

OM AND OHM

The religion of the future will be a cosmic religion.

Albert Einstein

What is the cosmic religion? It is the very first sound a baby makes when a gentle tap on its buttocks energises the tiny heart with its first beat.

This is the vibration that pulsates throughout the human body, our invisible thread that sounds the entire universe in a flash.

Ingeniously Panini and perhaps his co-grammarians figured out a way to interpret all these sounds through the use of language and numbers to resonate with the all-mighty 9.

I lean mainly towards Panini because the letters of his name reduce to 9 like love, source, deity and divine, sun and rays.

Heart too for the sound of it could do with another t.

If you wish to experience your heart beat in any part of your body meditate on energising all the cells of your body.

I have described the process under meditation in this book.

The *OM* sound, interpreted as AH OOO MMNN (999) or AUM, may have originated from the number 9 in the writing system of the Devanagari traditions of India.

According to history, 9 as we know it today, in its fourth stage of evolution, morphed to look like a 3 enclosed in a circle, like the modern-day OM. Somewhere along the OM's history, it was interpreted as meaning that everything in our lives is in threes.

Perhaps it is an interplay between 3 and 9 for:

- The Trimurti (39 = 3 deity), the trinity of Brahma, Vishnu, and Shiva in Hinduism
- God, eulogised through the eighteen Puranas (sacred writings) through divine stories
- Brahma, Vishnu, and Shiva, representing creation, preservation, and destruction
- The three ingredients in our make-up: truth, passion, and ignorance
- Time, space, and causation
- The three periods in our lives, represented by our month, day, and year of birth—each a third of our total human lifespan on earth
- The three states of consciousness: waking, dreams, and deep sleep
- The three stages to a human life: physical, psychological, and spiritual—each approximately a third of our lives if we are not stuck in the first two stages.

CHAPTER 32

SUN, OHM, IR, PHYSICS, EQUATE TO 9

> Everything is energy and that's all there is to it. Match the frequency of the reality you want and you cannot help but get that reality. It can be no other way. This is not philosophy. This is physics.
>
> Albert Einstein

In physics, *energy* is defined as 'the capacity or ability to do work mainly through the movement of objects, waves, and heat from one place or object to another or change from one form to another'.

The sun powers our universe through its heat and light; it even illuminates us intellectually and spiritually.

In Ohm's law for electric current, E stands for voltage, I stands for current (amps), and R stands for resistance. Current is in a state of flow, and resistance is the degree of the hardship faced by the power source.

The forcing of an electric current through an electrical circuit causes a dissipation of power in the circuitry (the design or planned design of the circuit).

Resistance is measured in ohms.

Joule is the unit of energy exerted, and calorie is the unit of energy as in heat (as in heat energy of exercise burns fat). Four joules equals one calorie.

CHAPTER 33

A DIVINE DESIGN

Divine is all Love in its essential nature, and Love is
Divine in its truthful expression.

Maharishi Mahesh Yogi

From all that has been discovered so far, it seems our system for
written and expressed communication was designed to be a constant
reminder of our connection to the divine.

It is very similar to how Sanskrit was systemised, with its rules
and grammar, in the Devanagari script in most parts of India. *Deva*
means 'heavenly'.

It seems English too is a sacred medium with an implied potency
for the inherent power in all our interactions. Our words may uplift
us or, conversely, embody a resistance to the flow of life.

CHAPTER 34

SUPPRESSION

But the human tongue is a beast that few can master.
It strains constantly to break out of its cage, and if it is not
tamed, it will run wild and cause you grief.

Unknown

If, for any reason, we are not convinced that we are always in the arms of providence, then it is time for some deep reflection. Perhaps we have been somehow influenced by our external circumstances, blinded to the knowledge that the self within all of us caters omnisciently and unequivocally for all humankind with wise benevolence.

We must look at life with a different perspective if we are frustrated in not living out our dreams. It will be due to our own inaction that suffering will be painfully inflicted on us.

Later we shall come to know compelling reasons we are always superstars of our own lives. Finally, we shall come to learn that humanity all along, through the mode of our communication in the language of alphabets and numbers, always animated our lives.

When we curtail our spirit connection, especially with our thinking and speaking, we endure more lows than highs, with many agitations. The natural flow of the divine, in its suppression, turns our body energy into a contracted, dense form according to the laws of physics. This is how we are manipulated by our thoughts and expressions to find an outlet in our ego.

CHAPTER 35

THE LITMUS TEST

The code to our divine connection lies in the following alphabet values:

A, J, S	= 1
B, K, T	= 2
C, L, U	= 3
D, M, V	= 4
E, N, W	= 5
F, O, X	= 6
G, P, Y	= 7
H, Q, Z	= 8
I, R	= 9.

The following equate to 9 or to the reduced value of 9: the I is the spirit or the self and also the ego of self-esteem.

All these words have divine connotations:

- aatma—soul or light of the Lord
- avatar—the incarnation of a Hindu deity
- Allah hu—a traditional Sufi chant meaning 'god' in Arabic and 'truth'
- Ah OOO Mmnn—the three basic sounds in language
- Aravat—*god* in Hebrew
- Budha—a deity in Hindu mythology (Puranic)

- deity—a god or goddess
- divine—of or like a god, or a god
- dharma—divine law fulfilled by observance of these laws
- ego—the spirit or god
- eimi—*ego eimi*, 'I exist' in Greek
- El Shaddai—one of the names of the God of Israel
- ego—I of self-importance or self-ignorance
- Gaia—goddess of earth
- Ganesh—a Hindu god of wisdom and learning, remover of obstacles
- gods—deities
- Govinda—a name of Krishna in Hinduism
- Hari Raamu—Sanskrit names for supreme beings
- Hari Krisna—Sanskrit names for supreme beings
- Gautama—known as the awakened one
- Hashem—a Hebrew term for 'God' (the Name)
- Khuda—the Iranian word for 'Lord' or 'God'
- mitzvah—Hebrew word that refers to precepts commanded by God
- mystics—could refer to those who know divine truths
- OM—a sacred sound and a spiritual icon in the Hindu religion; also used as a prayer and in mantras universally
- Puranas—ancient Hindu texts eulogising various deities
- saint—persons of exceptional holiness
- sanatana dharma —religiously ordained practices in Hinduism
- satsang—in the company of a guru or of the highest truths
- Shri Radhe—goddess of the universe
- saguna braama—the Absolute
- shaanti—invocation for peace
- Shivam—pertaining to Lord Shiva
- spirituals—Christian songs.

CHAPTER 36

GOD'S MY PHYSICS

> The important thing is not to stop questioning. Curiosity has its own reason for existence. One cannot help but be in awe when he contemplates the mysteries of eternity, of life, of the marvellous structure of reality. It is enough if one tries merely to comprehend a little of this mystery every day. Never lose a holy curiosity.

> Albert Einstein

Once again, we see the genius of Panini in being able to dazzle us with an array of scientific 9s strung together as if by a magician's wand through the divine sparklers from beneath the words. Is this how the *truth* is expressed—in a mystical 'flash of insight or revelation'?

Samsara refers to an eternal cycle of life, death, and reincarnation.

Samsara: Panini, sun, rays, source, origin, electrician, mathematician, geometry, physics, circuitry, breath, oxygen, engine, 36.9 degrees Celsius, current, mho, calorie, joule, carbons, ohm, resist.

Their equivalents:

- 9: 9, 9, 9, 9, 9, 9, 9, 9, 9, 9, 9, 9, 9, 9, 9, 9, 9, 9, 9, 9, 9
- Rishi, an inspired sage or poet
- &, by itself (it was the twenty-seventh letter of the alphabet).

CHAPTER 37

FLOW AND RESISTANCE

I, me, ego, god's talks and sums, love and lover, worry
and resist too, don't you see I am in all of them.

Devad

All life is encapsulated in the physics of the free-flow energy
current of the *I* in the IR and the resistance to the free flow, causing
suppressed energy in the *R* of the IR. This is likened to the spirit
within us wanting to express our creativity and the ego of self-
importance that hijacks our inner urge to express our ingenuity.

I hope the world gets to know our divinity as a powerful force
for all mankind to enshrine *love* in the temple of their hearts. All
our spoken and written mediums are perfumed with the universal
presence and embellished with sweet grace.

This is a monumental revelation of the power of divinity that
we must all respect for love and compassion to flourish on earth. All
living things are sacred.

CHAPTER 38

ADD TALKS & SUMS

9 9 27 9

'Hello, how are you, son?'
85336 865 195 763 165?
'Good, Dad, thanks.'
7664 414 281521.
'I am happy.'
9 14 81777.
'I love you, son.'
9 3645 763 165.
'I will see you later.'
9 5933 155 763 31259.

In the above conversation, the numeral values are sending vibrations electrically through the charged atmosphere. The 9s and words reduced to 9 communicate directly to all the nine members of the cosmos.

Just as the sun and its rays are directing their 9s to us and all other forms of life that enrich life on earth, we breathe out carbons and breathe in oxygen, and as we talk, we too are sending out 9s everywhere.

Our interaction with the gods, deities, the divine, the sun, and its rays is continuous. It is instantaneous communication. Our mass form conceptualises time and space, but actually it is our spirit that is doing the talking. The messages we are sending from the standpoint of the spirit is compassionate and loving, but through our body limitations, we cannot see beyond the words we utter.

Our spirit is the observer, always looking out for us, but the subject and object sometimes act as one or as two, depending what thoughts are going through our minds.

When we are conscious of our actions and their consequences for our well-being and health, we align with the source. If we pander to the dictates of our ego, then our words are in opposition of the self's appeal on our behalf; we incur pain and suffering.

This is how meditation was prescribed in almost all cultures in some form or the other to limit the noise and be quiet. When no thoughts appear and no words are spoken, we effortlessly jump into the oneness in and around us; a connection is made that seems timeless and spaceless.

All the good 9s are with us for us to enjoy and to have fun with the play of life. Mantras can be very effective to lift our vibratory levels to resonate with all the names and words that are all 9s, such as this universal mantra, *Hari Krisna, Hari Krisna, Krisna Krisna, Hari Hari, Hari Raamu, Hari Raamu, Raamu, Raamu, Hari Hari.* These 9s, sixteen of them, are tuning in *source, deity, divine, love,* and *lover* too.

It is important to watch our relationships with words so they contribute to our well-being. Words that contain the ego part of our lives, represented by the R, are to be avoided, as they don't have a positive effect. Those that contain IR in that order and that have a flow-and-resist factor may not serve our purpose. On the other hand, those with RI have resistance and flow but best be avoided.

The best outcomes are those conversations that are made up of vocabulary that, as far as possible, are without the R and where the number values more or less sync with 9. Even with the names we make up or suggest for anyone, especially babies, we should definitely avoid the R being part of the names. However, if a word which has the R adds up to 9, perhaps it could be okay to use.

CHAPTER 39

AN APPRECIATION

PANINI FOR THE MAGIC OF ENGLISH

Panini grammatically, sharpened, enhanced
mathematician and electrician lives in the IR of our lives.

Devad

Panini spells 9 and makes him sit amongst those in the region of the divine. He grammatically sharpened and enhanced the English language as a mathematician. Through a brilliant configuration of the letters, his arrangement and organisation to make them match the numbers 1 to 9 in ascending order is beyond belief. The electrician in him revealed the human ego construct long before the IR in Ohm's law was made known—sheer brilliance.

Legend has it that Panini overheard an astrologer, his father's good friend, tell his father reluctantly and with sadness that the boy's palm lacked the line of learning. However, Panini's interest in studying did not discourage him but stirred up his resolve to do something about it.

Little Panini asked the guest where on his palm the missing line of learning was meant to be. With this knowledge, he ran out to the backyard. Panini returned after his attempt to make the missing line with a sharp stone left him with a bleeding palm stripe, which prompted his dad to vow to make him a scholar.

Sometime later, the story goes, after a tiring day of doing much reading, which he was devoted to, he fell asleep. He awoke to the sound of drumbeats and caught a glimpse of Lord Shiva, who blessed Panini and disappeared into the blazing light. I recall my Tamil schoolteacher relating a similar story to us many times when I was a young boy.

There is no doubt that Panini could have had such divine visitation, for no mortal mind could conjure up the synchronicity of the universe's mystical designs within and all around us by the way the divine springs to life to play with us through the English language. The spirit of 9 never ceases to show itself to us, endlessly teasing us to awake from our long and deep slumber.

Panini vibrates in the rich tapestry of our lives every moment, alphanumerically, when thousands of words resonate with the 9, sending sparks of divine love also etched in his name.

Chapter 40

ACKNOWLEDGEMENTS

9—the perfect, the whole, the complete, impregnable,
changes all but itself never changes.

Devad

Now we know English was always the voice of God, and perhaps all our lives from now on have taken a giant step spiritually that is going to bring the world much closer than ever before.

We feel grateful and thankful for all the good in our daily lives. We thank all those who, through their humbleness and generosity of heart, express vibrations of love, kindness, charity, and compassion for the benefit of all and everything on this earth. We thank those too who, through your thoughts, words (spoken and written), and actions, create a better place for all.

BIBLIOGRAPHY

Biography [website], 'Nikola Tesla Biography' (A&E Television Networks).

Bite Size Physics [website] <bitesizephysics.com>

Cardona, G., *Panini: A Survey of Research* (Paris, 1976).

Chidbhavananda, Srimath Swami, tr., *The Bhagavad Gita*.

Coward, Harold G., *The Sphota Theory of Language: A Philosophical Analysis* (Delhi: Motilal Banarsidass, 1980).

Franklin, Michael J., ed, *Sir William Jones: Selected Poetical and Prose Works* (University of Wales Press, 1995), 365–370.

Goodreads [website] <goodreads.com>

Google [website] <google.com>

Habits for Wellbeing [website], '20 quotes to Inspire Connectedness'. <www.habitsforwellbeing.com>

HitXP [website] <hitxp.com>

Ifrah, Georges, *From One to Zero: A Universal History of Numbers* (Viking, 1985).

ILoveIndia [website] <iloveindia.com>

Joseph, G. G., *The Crest of the Peacock: Non-European Roots of Mathematics* (London, 1991).

Macdonell, Arthur Anthony, 'Chapter 16: Sanskrit Literature and the West', *A History of Sanskrit Literature* (1900).

Ohm, Georg Simon, *Die Galvanische Kette, Mathematisch Bearbeitet*, (Berlin: T. H. Riemann, 1827).

Omniglot [website], 'Devanagari Alphabet'. <omniglot.com/writing/Devanagari>

Osborn, David, 'The History of Numbers', Vedic Sciences.

Sivananda, Sri Swami, *Bhagavad Gita for Busy People* (Himalayas, India: The Divine Life Society). <www.dlshq.org/ ≥

Stanley, Bessie Anderson, 'Success', *Brown Book Magazine* (Boston, 1904)

.Sathguru, 'Yugas – Tides of Time'. <youtube.com>

Wikipedia [website], 'Ohm's Law'. Accessed 2 April 2018.

Wikipedia [website], '9'. Accessed 14 May 2018.

Wikipedia [website], 'Panini'. Accessed 9 July 2018.

YouTube [website] <youtube.com>

Zero-Wise [website] <zero-wise.com>

INDEX

ABOUT THE AUTHOR

This inspiring and inspirational revolutionary approach to life is the culmination of years of searching to unravel the missing ingredient in my quest for total fulfilment. Aquarius's star has risen, for times of great changes in the world are afoot, as my soul could not resist this deep longing in me. So with divine help, it led me to itself to reveal how we are all inextricably key players in our expressions, forever reaching out to the universe's love and compassion from behind our very words to satisfy all our desires. Inevitably, all our yearnings sparkle and shine in an array of invocations mirrored in the perfection of the immutable, unchangeable, euphoric 9. All our souls seek what we promised. Panini will be smiling because his genius has risen once again to shine his unmatched brilliance on us.

About the Book

This is the most valuable handbook you will need for your journey home, the road that you promised your soul that you would remember to take.

The English language underwent many changes in its evolution, and finally, you will get to know that it is the centrepiece of yourself and those you dearly cherish. Hush, don't say too much before you understand what it is you wish to convert to words. You may be a magician and act the fool, but the universe knows your games and will gladly play with you too.

Printed in the United States
By Bookmasters